TIME FOR A CHANGE

Did you know that—

- In 1990, Americans were working 160 more hours a year than they did in 1970—about one extra month per year.

- A life insurance company survey shows stress at work has more than doubled in a recent five-year period.

- 57% of middle managers routinely work an extra 6 to 20 hours of overtime each week.

- *The Wall Street Journal* reports that because of fax, cellular phones, and electronic mail many executives and managers feel they never get away from their jobs.

- 63% of Americans want more free time to spend as they please.

DON'T YOU?—

WORK A 4-HOUR DAY

WORK A 4-HOUR DAY

ACHIEVING BUSINESS EFFICIENCY ON YOUR OWN TERMS

Arthur K. Robertson and
William Proctor

AVON BOOKS NEW YORK

AVON BOOKS
A division of
The Hearst Corporation
1350 Avenue of the Americas
New York, New York 10019

Copyright © 1994 by Arthur Robertson
Published by arrangement with William Morrow and Company, Inc.
Library of Congress Catalog Card Number: 93-8365
ISBN: 0-380-72627-0

The William Morrow edition contains the following Library of Congress Cataloging in Publication Data:

Robertson, Arthur K.
  Work a four-hour day / Arthur K. Robertson and William Proctor.
    p.   cm.
1. Leisure.   2. Time management.   I. Proctor, William.   II. Title.
HD4904.6.R62   1994
640'.43—dc20
                                                            93-8365
                                                            CIP

First Avon Books Printing: March 1996

AVON TRADEMARK REG. U.S. PAT. OFF. AND IN OTHER COUNTRIES, MARCA REGISTRADA, HECHO EN U.S.A.

Printed in the U.S.A.

RA   10   9   8   7   6   5   4   3   2   1

Contents

Chapter One

What Is the Four-Hour Day?

Once upon a time, in the early years of the twentieth century, economic pundits predicted that by the 1990s, leisure time would abound in the United States. Through technology, increased productivity, and the pressure of labor unions, we would be able to work less and play more. We'd have extra time to pursue a wide variety of personal interests—with no boss or organization to control us.

In the minds of some of these visionaries, the *four-hour day* became one of the symbols of the American Conquest of Time. The idea was that before the end of the millennium, it would be possible to get all your work done in four hours a day, or twenty hours a week—*not* the eight-hour days and forty-hour weeks that by World War II had become the standard for the average worker. You'd be paid the same, or even more, but you'd have to work only half the time.

The potential benefits of working four hours for a full day's pay seemed staggering. If you allowed for eight hours of sleep per day, you'd still be left with twelve hours to use as you pleased—enjoying your family, writing a novel, reading a long-postponed book, or lying on a beach!

WHATEVER HAPPENED
TO THE FOUR-HOUR DAY?

Obviously, something has gone wrong with this idealized, more-play-less-work scenario. Take a few moments to conduct your own reality check. How many people do *you* know who put in four hours—or anything close to it—for a full day's wage?

There are a few out there who might qualify, including a handful of elite consultants, investors, writers, or semi-retired entrepreneurs. One case in point: since the 1970s, Sir John Templeton, the founder of the highly successful Templeton group of mutual funds, has devoted only half his working time to his investments, which he manages from an estate in the Bahamas. The other half of his hours go into religious and charitable activities. But there aren't many John Templetons around.

By almost any standard we've failed miserably to reduce our work time and to increase real leisure time. Certainly, we're light-years away from achieving the ideal of the four-hour day of work, as the following facts about American work habits demonstrate.

- Since about 1970, the normal American work week, which had dropped to about thirty-nine hours, began to go up again, according to Harvard researcher Juliet Schor. By 1990, Americans were working more than 160 additional hours each year—about one extra month per year.

- Stress at work more than doubled in a recent five-year period, according to a survey by the Northwestern Mutual Life Insurance Company.

- In the July–September fiscal quarter of 1992, over-time pay among city workers in New York City hit a two-year high.

- Only one third of middle managers routinely work

forty to forty-five hours a week; 57 percent have their noses to the grindstone for an extra six to twenty hours; and 6 percent report they work more than sixty hours weekly, according to a 1992 survey by Priority Management, a Seattle consulting firm.

- A 1992 Gallup poll found that 57 percent of Americans say they have too little time for hobbies; 57 percent want more time to relax; 48 percent want more time with their spouses; and 39 percent desire more time with their children.

- Between 1973 and 1987, the average American's free time shrank from 26.2 hours per week to 16.6 hours per week, according to a Louis Harris survey.

- Because of such technological breakthroughs as the fax, cordless and car phones, and electronic mail, many executives and managers feel they are so surrounded by their work that they are unable to separate their job from their home life, says a 1991 *Wall Street Journal* report.

- A 1991 Hilton Hotels Time Values Survey found that 66 percent of Americans wanted to have more free time to spend any way they pleased; and 38 percent cut back on sleep to make more time.

- In the same Hilton survey, an astounding 70 percent of those earning $30,000 a year or more declared that they would give up a day's pay each week for an extra day of time.

The main problem we face is not just the burden of having to work. After all, up to a point, most people *like* to be productive or to become occupied in some meaningful task. But dissatisfaction arises when we find we have to spend *too much time on work that we dislike*; or when we have *too many duties to accomplish in far too little time*; or when we *misuse the leisure time that is available to us*. Our dilemma can be summed up in terms of two basic challenges that we must overcome if we are to achieve a four-hour day in our lives:

Challenge #1: The actual increase in work time.

Part of the problem we face seems to be an *actual* increase in time spent on the job or working around the house. As the Harris survey and the Schor study mentioned above demonstrate, since the early 1970s we appear to be spending, on average, an extra month each year on our work. So anyone who wants to achieve a four-hour day *must*, somehow, reduce the number of hours he or she devotes to daily labor.

Challenge #2: Maximizing the use of leisure time.

Along with an *actual* excess of work time, you may feel dissatisfied because there just don't *seem* to be enough hours in the day after work for personal business and pleasure.

To put this another way, many people feel dissatisfied because of a *perceived loss* of their leisure time. What are the reasons for this perception? Some possibilities include the increased pace of life, the demands of two-career families, and the burgeoning choices that fragment free time. These and similar factors have made many people sense that they have less extra time than they really do.

One exhausted couple told us that they had no time just to relax after taking one of their children to a gymnastics meet, carting another to a basketball game, and then catching the last part of a party being thrown by some of their friends.

"*We don't seem to have time for anything anymore,*" the husband said.

Yet when he actually calculated the non-work time available that Saturday, he found they had nearly twelve hours at their disposal! The problem was that this couple had crammed far too many activities into a limited time frame and had transformed a potentially leisurely weekend into a personal pressure cooker. In many ways, they had chosen worthwhile activities for their leisure hours. Their mistake was that they had picked too many of them!

There's also a widespread tendency to *misuse* non-work hours by selecting time-wasting activities to fill the leisure period. Excessive television watching is one of the worst offenders. Professor John Robinson of the University of Maryland notes that the TV consumes 37 percent of the free time of American women and 39 percent of the free time of American men.

Other activities may fall into the time-wasting category for you: constantly going to movies; wandering around the local mall; shopping for items you don't really need; making excessive preparations before attending or hosting parties; choosing to wait in long lines; or just spending a lot of time trying to decide what to do. Making decisions about how to use our free time can, quite literally, take hours when we're confronted by a variety of consumer choices. Most people aren't particularly happy or satisfied when they devote so much time to TV or other time-wasters, but they have fallen into habits that cause them to squander the non-work hours available to them. A considerable amount of free time may be available; it just may not be utilized in a way that is consistent with one's values or goals in life.

Clearly, as a society, we're not even close to the relaxed freedom of the four-hour day. But is there some way that *you personally* can buck these all-work, no-play trends and achieve *your own* four-hour day?

IS IT REALLY POSSIBLE FOR <u>YOU</u>?

At this point, you may be thinking, "This four-hour-day business is all fantasy. I have a regular job with a boss who requires my presence for eight or more hours every day. There's no way I can change that!"

Or you may object, "I have children to care for, in

addition to my career. Any thought of a four-hour day is ridiculous!''

Or, "I'm trying to build my own business. It's impossible for an entrepreneur to do that in only four hours a day."

Contrary to what you may think, it's possible for *anyone* to achieve—or at least come close to—some version of a four-hour working day. In more precise terms, here's what we mean by the term *four-hour day*, and what we want to encourage you to shoot for:

- If you're employed full-time outside your home, you can accomplish all the job-related work you need to accomplish in no more than four hours. (You'll first learn how to reduce your working time to four hours. Then, we'll help you deal with the issue of how to handle your boss.)

- If your main responsibilities are to supervise a household, you can accomplish all those tasks in no more than four hours.

- If you have both a full-time job outside the home *and* household responsibilities, you can do the outside work in no more than four hours and the household work in no more than two hours.

As you'll soon understand, the four-hour day is, indeed, quite possible. But the journey to this goal must take you well outside the usual path trod by typical time-management books.

HOW YOU CAN ACHIEVE YOUR OWN FOUR-HOUR DAY

Your quest for the four-hour day—the fulfillment of that elusive goal of significantly less work and more leisure time—should *not* begin simply with trying to become better organized.

Most of us have read books and magazine articles that advocate a variety of time-saving tips. These may teach you to increase your efficiency in handling your mail and paperwork, drastically reduce procrastination, and improve your overall productivity. But you may have found that no matter how hard you try, you simply can't succeed in incorporating these suggestions permanently into your behavior patterns. Or, after taking such measures, you may find that you actually have even *less* free time, and considerably *more* time pressure, than you had when you started!

Traditional time management techniques certainly can play a role in helping you achieve your own personal four-hour day. In fact, we'll be discussing some of the most helpful of these methods later in this book. But to make these practical measures really work for you, it's essential to transform your basic approach to time. To this end, in the following pages we'll explore:

- The different ways of perceiving time—and techniques you can use to slow it down or speed it up in your own life.

- How your use of time interacts with your personal priorities and values, and ways your basic beliefs can enhance your experience of time.

- Tools for discovering your *personal time dimension*, or the emotional, physical, and spiritual rhythms that determine how you operate most effectively and enjoyably during a typical day.

- The technique of *time analysis*—a highly practical and revealing exercise that will allow you to determine exactly where your minutes go every day, and how you can reorganize your life by formulating your own *time budget*.

- Ways to enjoy and use *transition time*, or those minutes and hours that act as necessary buffers between different periods of intense activity or work.

- How to overcome *time barriers*, such as procrastination, unnecessary meetings, and inefficient paperwork.

- Guidelines for developing the three basic speed skills—fast writing, fast reading, and effective listening.

- Tactics that will enable you to fight effectively for control over your own time.

Now, the moment has arrived to take the first important step in your quest for the four-hour day—to evaluate and transform your basic view of time and its possibilities.

Chapter Two

An Armchair Guide to Time Travel

What is time?

This question, the first that confronts us in our quest for the four-hour day, has been asked many times by philosophers, scientists, and theologians. Even the average person, who is constantly under the pressure of daily demands and deadlines, may occasionally wonder: *Why am I always under such time pressure? What is this force that seems to direct my life and hold me unrelentingly in its power?* Some assume that if you can understand what time is—if you can somehow quantify or analyze it—you can control or escape it. Yet all too often, those questioning the meaning of time conclude as Saint Augustine did: "What then is time? If no one asks me, I know that it is. If I wish to explain it to him who asks me, I do not know."

It certainly is difficult to arrive at a satisfactory definition or understanding of time with our limited human vocabulary. In many ways, the implications of time press us to the very outer edges of what our minds can conceive. Still, time explorers from ancient days to the present have pieced together some important insights that may help you in your search for your own four-hour day.

9

A TOUCH OF TIME TRAVEL

The first thing to understand is that working long hours and being under constant time pressure isn't necessarily part of the natural state of being human. People in the ancient world weren't as driven on a moment-to-moment basis by time as we are. Although they lacked our technological and medical advantages, there is evidence that many of them, who lived in areas with plenty of game and edible vegetation, did less work and had more leisure time than we do. Indeed, anthropological studies of "primitive" jungle tribes, bushmen, and island peoples around the world today indicate that many work four hours or fewer each day.

The lack of time pressure among early and primitive peoples is reflected in their slowness to develop precise methods for identifying and measuring years, months, seasons, and shorter periods, such as days or hours. It's been said that the calendar is the means human beings have used to divide the flow of their time into units that fit the demands of their society. *The fewer demands, the less need for a precise, detailed calendar.* So as you're pondering your own schedule and the possibility of a four-hour day, don't think you're locked into an immutable system that's a requirement for all humans.

How the calendar signals change. Beginning in about the third millennium B.C., the needs of society started to change. As agriculture became more sophisticated, farmers found they had to forecast the best times of the year to plant and harvest crops. Also, those in other occupations had already begun to see an advantage to knowing something about the seasons. Hunters had probably already found that they could expect wild flocks and herds to move about at certain times of the year. As towns and cities grew up, merchants and tradespeople discovered they had to arrange their schedules to accommodate growing numbers of customers, who had their own deadlines to meet. These needs increased the demand for better calendars.

In 46 B.C., Julius Caesar instituted the Julian calendar, a reform by the astronomer Sosigenes of all previous calendars. This new standard established the year at 365.25 days, and added an extra day every fourth February to compensate for a slight mathematical deviation from the precise solar year. The demands were increasing to make the measurement of time more and more precise—*a direct response to the economic complexity that was exerting increasing pressure on the average citizen*. The Julian calendar was used throughout the Western world for the next 1,600 years, until it was replaced in the sixteenth century by the even more precise Gregorian calendar, which we use today. (According to the Gregorian calendar, the length of the solar year is 365.2422 days. This results in a discrepancy of 3.12 days every 400 years.)

THE PRESSURE COOKER OF PRECISION TIME

As the measurement of time steadily became more exact, business magnates, politicians, and religious leaders soon saw that the day had to be subdivided. If you were going to operate your life and business as efficiently as the next guy, you also had to know the particular *hour* of the day.

So inventors were pressed to come up with an increasingly complex and more accurate series of sundials, water clocks, and other devices, until the first mechanical clock was developed in the early fourteenth century. The portable clock, or watch, came along during the Renaissance, and pendulums increased precision of the timepieces. We were well on our way to the modern conception of time—what we've chosen to call *precision time*—and all the personal pressures that go along with it.

Precision time involves a detailed and exact scheduling of the events and obligations of each day. Meetings are put on the agenda for a certain hour, and
participants are expected to be in their seats, ready to
go, precisely at the designated moment. Deadlines are
set for the completion of certain segments of a person's
work, and if those deadlines aren't met, there may be
consequences. You're expected to get to work "on
time," and you're only allowed to leave after a certain
hour. Even leisure activities are driven by the clock.
Children's soccer, basketball, or baseball games must
start by a certain hour, or the officials will declare a
forfeit or default. There's a check-in time and a check-
out time for hotels and the resorts where you spend
your vacation. And you'd better be down for dinner
at many hotels during a specific period or you may
not eat!

In some ways, Benjamin Franklin may be said to have
signaled the start of our era when he said in his *Advice
to a Young Tradesman*, "Time is money." With the ad-
vent of the Industrial Revolution in the eighteenth and
nineteenth centuries, manufacturers and other employers
drove their workers to labor longer and longer hours. Precise, sophisticated timekeeping devices, such as clocks
with second hands and alarms, allowed bosses to maintain
control over their subordinates. Bells or whistles would
signal the exact second when work was to begin or end.
Later, time-imprinting clocks were developed which required the worker to "punch in" and "out" when he went
on and off the job. Twelve- to fourteen-hour-days were
common in that period. This oppressive situation, which
Charles Dickens and other social critics of the period railed
against, may represent the low point in the history of
human work—and the farthest swing of the labor pendu-

lum away from the four-hour day. In response to these pressures, workers banded together to force their bosses to provide better working conditions, including shorter hours of work.

Today, the accelerating pace of life and technology continue to exert pressure for split-second scheduling and timing. Digital clocks and watches can display fractions of a second that we can only *hope* will never be of any practical use to the ordinary worker. Those timing athletic events have felt it necessary to measure human speed by the hundredth or thousandth of a second. Now scientists are using even more precise devices that measure down to the microsecond (one millionth of a second) and even the nanosecond (one billionth of a second!).

Clearly, there has been a disturbing deterioration in the relationship between human beings and their concept of time. Far from being a relaxed, general measurement of the flow of seasons and festivals—a tool to *enhance* life—time is too often our master or enemy. We are driven to be at the right place, at the right time, whether we like the idea or not. Yet in most cases, we don't know why we're running at breakneck speed. For that matter, we're often not even sure of our final destination.

What can you do to take charge of your time and actually reduce your working hours? Is it really possible to resist these high-pressure time trends and move toward some version of the four-hour day?

Yes, it is possible. But first, it's necessary to revise your basic approach to time.

TAKE ANOTHER LOOK AT YOUR UNDERSTANDING OF TIME

The increasing complexity of our economy has made the development of exact timekeeping devices and systems inevitable. But step back for a moment from your daily pressure cooker and take another look at the role of time in your life. You may find that a large part of the time oppression you feel stems from one or more fallacies about the way you *conceive* of time.

Fallacy #1: Time is an inflexible container.

Sir Isaac Newton is often cited as the main source for this view. He conceived of time as a kind of hard, inflexible container that held the universe and all change within the universe. Time was an absolute, unchanging entity that was independent of the physical universe. In this view, there's nothing that human beings can do to shape or change time. Those who complain, "There are only so many hours in the day," are affirming this outlook.

What's wrong with the container idea? Albert Einstein and his followers have blown it to smithereens with their arguments that time *cannot* be understood independently of space. These modern "relativity" thinkers see a four-dimensional space-time continuum, in which the measurement and flow of time is bound up with the speed of light. Time, including the process of aging, actually can move at different rates, depending on the speed at which you're traveling. To explain this concept, physicists have posited what they call the "paradox of the twins"—an illustration of Einstein's special theory of relativity.

Assume that there are identical twins, one of whom stays on earth while the other embarks on a trip into space. The stationary twin will age like the rest of us, according to ordinary earth time. But the traveling twin will age more slowly—*much* more slowly if his speed in space approaches the speed of light. One month of space travel at almost the speed of light would amount to ten years of earth time! The reason: according to Einstein's special theory of relativity, which is now generally accepted, time for the astronaut twin will actually expand or slow down as he moves at high speeds through space.

In other words, there are two separate and measurable

systems of time at work here: one for the earthling, and the other for the space traveler.

A space-time lesson. What's the lesson for those of us who will never experience travel in space? Time is a *relative* framework, or concept, in our lives, *not* an inflexible container. So don't allow yourself to start out with the assumption that you only have a certain number of hours or minutes to accomplish a task or to make it through the day successfully. Instead, think like the twins separated by space travel. Always be alert to ways that your time can be expanded or contracted—and to possibilities for understanding or viewing your time in a more productive or exciting way. You'll learn some practical applications of this insight in Chapter 4.

Fallacy #2: Time is outside my mind.

In fact, there is much evidence that in some respects, time is *not* outside the human mind. Instead, the rate at which time passes is largely a matter of personal perception.

Various studies have shown, for instance, that:

- Continuous, smooth execution of a task seems to take less time than activity marked by many stops, starts, and interruptions.

- Activity done with great motivation seems to take a shorter period of time than activity done without motivation.

- Drugs such as hashish, mescaline, and other stimulants make time seem to go slowly, perhaps because they produce so many more sensations than are normally received by the body and mind.

- Drugs such as depressants and anesthetics make time appear to go quickly, probably because they reduce the normal number of sensations.

- Raising the temperature of the body may cause the overheated or feverish person to underestimate the amount of time that has passed. (That is, time will seem to move more slowly for him than for those with a normal temperature.) Conversely, a lower body temperature should make time seem to move more quickly.

Obviously, if you placed a stopwatch next to the people who were experiencing these different conditions, the same objective time would pass for all. But there is a dimension of time that reaches beyond the objective realm and into subjective, inner perceptions. A part of time is, indeed, in your mind.

Some lessons in perception. What lessons can we learn from these points about the perception of time?

You'll find you have less of a struggle with time constraints if you can find ways (1) to get involved in uninterrupted, smoothly moving activities; and (2) to become more motivated.

Caution: You should *not* try to combine drugs with your everyday activities, nor should you try to raise or lower your body temperature! These examples were only included to illustrate ways that the mind's perceptions of time can be altered. Current evidence indicates that the use of drugs or other means tends to hinder, rather than help, the efficiency of the mind and body.

You'll learn more about establishing a smooth flow to your schedule and enhancing your motivation in Chapters 5 through 7.

Fallacy #3: Time is the ultimate authority in my life.

Too often, we live our entire lives—day after day, year after year—without thinking about where we are going. The image of the treadmill, or of the endless highway, gives us a sense that the duties and tasks of life are relentless and ultimately meaningless. Certainly, specific occupational responsibilities have to be met. But, ultimately, the journey we're on doesn't mean much because we spend our lives responding to the demands of time, rather than *using that time as a tool to take us where we want to go*.

If you've felt yourself falling into this trap of being controlled by time, the chances are you have allowed values and priorities outside yourself to take over your life. Remember, time is nothing more than a means of measuring activity or motion. It's only one dimension of reality, along with height, width, and depth. Time is not an authoritative, omnipotent force in itself—unless you allow it to become one.

There are at least four sources of authority in your life that may determine the extent to which you control your time, or it controls you.

The authority of other people. We all order our lives to some extent according to the demands and needs of other people. If a member of your family needs your help or wants to talk with you, the chances are you'll drop whatever you're doing and respond. Or if your boss says she needs a report turned in by a certain deadline, you'll probably do your best to meet that requirement.

There's nothing wrong with being responsive to others; in fact, it's impossible to maintain human relationships without some significant degree of sensitivity. The problem arises if *all* or *most* of your time is taken up by the demands and dictates of others. In such situations, other people become a kind of "god," or ultimate source of authority over your time. This situation always leads to dissatisfactions, anxieties, or other emotional and spiritual problems.

The authority of shoulds and oughts. Everyone has a set of *shoulds* and *oughts* that drive his or her activities and take up time. Some are admirable, such as the feeling that we *should* help the poor or that we *ought* to comfort an unhappy friend or relative. But other *shoulds* and *oughts* are more likely to become time-wasters.

You might think, "I really *should* cook my own turkey rather than buy one already cooked at the supermarket." If you give in to that *should*, you'll also have to devote a great deal of your time to the extra cooking. Or you might think, "I *ought* to spend an extra couple of hours working on this project tonight so that I can be sure to meet the deadline tomorrow." If you give in to that *ought*, you'll automatically cut into your free, non-work, family time.

The authority of accidental time. One of the most common ways that we relinquish authority over our own time is not to think or plan at all, but just to *react*. If you are mainly a reactor, you'll find that your life is controlled not by any overriding, well-thought-through purpose, but by "accidental time," or events and demands that just happen to cross your path during the day. One woman, whose entire life had become a series of time accidents, recently experienced a day that went something like this:

She got up at her usual time and commuted to work. When she arrived at her job, she immediately started working on a project that was due the next day; but within minutes, she was interrupted by a friend who wanted to chat. She finally returned to the project about fifteen minutes later, but by then her boss put some other assignments on her desk. So she put her big project aside and did a couple of the new assignments, without paying any attention to the fact that they weren't due until the following week.

The entire day proceeded with one interruption after the other, yet this woman never questioned seriously what her priorities should be for her day's work. At the end of the day, she had made almost no progress on the project that was due the following morning. But when she was asked to accompany some friends to a party that night, she accepted because, as she said, "I've worked so hard today, I deserve a little time off."

Of course, the project that was due the next day didn't get finished. This woman had been controlled by a series of "time accidents," or choices that she made without thinking seriously about the consequences.

The authority of authentic personal priorities. All of the above three factors—other people, *shoulds* and *oughts*, and time accidents—will at some point play a role in your choice about how you use your time. But the primary driving force behind how you organize your day and your life *must be a clear-cut set of personal priorities*.

Achieving the four-hour day isn't possible unless you have a profound understanding of your life goals and a personal vision of what you want your future to be. That's why the adventure of the four-hour day must begin in your mind and spirit.

Chapter Three

The Adventure Begins in Your Mind

In the popular movie *City Slickers* this provocative interchange takes place as Billy Crystal, the "city slicker" on vacation from his high-powered urban job, and Jack Palance, the tough old cowhand, ride the range together:

CRYSTAL: "What's the meaning of life?"
PALANCE: "Just one thing."
CRYSTAL: "What's that?"
PALANCE: "That's what you've got to figure out."

The remainder of the movie depicts Crystal in a variety of physical and emotional challenges that eventually lead him to conclude that the "one thing" in his life is his family. This celluloid parable points the way toward the first and most important objective in your quest for control over your time and achievement of the four-hour day: *setting clear priorities in your life.*

For Crystal, family took a priority over career. Other people may choose another set of priorities, such as a form of volunteer service or religious devotion. In any event, the choice of some kind of priority, principle, or faith as a guide to live by is essential—for a number of reasons.

WHAT'S SO IMPORTANT ABOUT PRIORITIES?

Time, as we've seen in the previous chapter, is a hard concept to describe. It may have different meanings and measurements and may seem to proceed at different rates and rhythms, depending on your subjective state when you're having a time-defined experience. Fortunately, your perception and use of time doesn't have to be subject to accident or chance. You can control the flow, pace, and enjoyment of your time *if* you order your actions, commitments, and responsibilities according to the main priorities in your life.

What do we mean by *priorities*? A real-life illustration should help explain.

How Tom got his time on track. Tom was a highly educated businessman in the pharmaceutical industry, with both an M.B.A. and a graduate degree in medical science. His professional credentials had opened up many career doors, including a high management position in his firm and frequent invitations to write for technical publications in his field. He was also much in demand as a speaker to groups employed in the prescription drug business.

Tom's problem was that he tried to take advantage of almost every professional opportunity that came his way. That meant that he spent an average of ten hours a day in his office, and then continued to work late into the night at home.

The demands on him were compounded by the fact that he was married and had a nine-year-old son who was active in sports and other extracurricular activities. Being a conscientious father, Tom tried to attend his son's athletic events as well as help him with his homework many nights. He also strove to be attentive to his wife, assist in the household chores (she held a part-time job), *and* participate in committee and service work at his church. Needless to say, there weren't enough hours in the day for Tom to accomplish all the tasks he had set for himself. He was constantly shortchanging himself on his sleep; he almost always had to leave some family responsibility or goal undone; and he found himself becoming more irritable and anxious.

It would have been easy to tell Tom, "Just give up a few of the things you're doing, and you'll have plenty of time." In fact, that's exactly what one friend did advise. And because he was becoming desperate, Tom did make an attempt to cut back on some of his publications and speaking assignments, to reduce his commitments at his church, and even to limit his outings with his son. But this solution didn't really help. Because everything he was doing seemed equally important, he regretted giving up the opportunities he had bypassed. Also, when new possibilities presented themselves, either at the office or at home, his tendency was still to take them on. His rationalization: "I can always cut back again if the pressure becomes too intense." In fact, however, he didn't cut back, but just returned to the same, overcommitted position that had been his downfall before.

Tom's main problem was that, unlike Billy Crystal's character in *City Slickers*, he had failed to find the "one thing" that should be a priority in his life. He was giving equal weight to many things, and as a result, he found himself at loose ends, with his time almost totally out of control.

Fortunately, Tom found a solution to his dilemma. A trusted friend whom he knew through his church suggested that he think of his life in terms of a simple sequence of three descending priorities: "It should be God-family-career, in that order," the confidant said.

The "God" priority, the man explained, didn't mean Tom had to devote most of his time to church activities: rather, he should focus on the faith, ethics, and principles that were the essence of his religion. Tom was encouraged to measure *every* time-related decision he had to make against his basic personal values and philosophy of life.

Those decisions about the use of his time had to be made in a way that was *consistent* or *congruent* with his world view.

For example, one of the reasons that he chose that particular God-family-career sequence for ordering his life was that he believed, profoundly, that his relationships with his family members should take precedence over his career. In effect, his positioning of his family in second place in his life (after God) was an article of religious faith with him. In practical terms, this meant that if he had a choice between doing some extra, job-related work or spending time with his wife and son, he should almost always choose the latter.

When Tom first tried organizing his time this way, he felt he was venturing into unfamiliar territory. He occasionally wondered, "Am I holding my career back when I choose not to do this article or give that speech?" But soon, he became entirely comfortable arranging his life according to these priorities. Most important of all, he felt a sense of inner peace, or "rightness," that his life—and his use of time—were finally on the right track.

HOW A WISE SET OF PRIORITIES CAN TRANSFORM YOUR TIME

If you begin your search for the four-hour day by first identifying and then following your personal priorities, you'll quickly note several benefits. These positive features will signal that you're well on your way to improving your productivity, enhancing your leisure hours, and, if you desire, reducing your work time. Here are some of the most important changes you'll experience:

Change #1: You'll handle stress better.

Much of the stress in our lives arises because the things we *do* are out of sync with what we *believe*. To put it another way, there is a *lack of congruence*, or consistency, between our actions and the basic values, priorities, or world view that we know is right for us.

Sometimes this incongruent state may occur by design: you may know that a certain type of action is inconsistent with your beliefs but go ahead with it anyhow. At other times, a lack of congruence may arise by accident, or at least without any conscious intent. For example, it's easy to slip into patterns of time use by reacting to the immediate pressures of life rather than planning your actions in advance so that you can avoid heading in undesirable directions.

With congruence present in your use of time, you'll find you have less guilt about not doing the things that you feel, deep down, you "should" do. Also, you'll be less likely to worry or be distracted because of a sense that you're not living in a way that's consistent with your belief system. Finally, your energy level will improve significantly; stress is one of the greatest enemies of physical and emotional vigor and well-being.

Change #2: You'll be more productive.

With your priorities and actions in harmony, you'll not only experience less stress and worry; you'll also become more productive and efficient in your use of time. Among other things, you will feel less of a tendency to shift back and forth between tasks and responsibilities—a habit that causes you to lose the efficiency that accompanies continuous flow of work.

Ally, an associate in a large eastern law firm, found that she was constantly "at loose ends" because of the variety and volume of work that the senior partners gave her. She would be handed an assignment by one partner that required long hours of research and was due by a certain date; a day later, she would be told by another partner to write an extensive memo for him on an entirely different topic. At times, she became completely immobilized because she couldn't decide how to proceed with her responsibilities. The demands of those above her, which were not well coordinated, caused tremendous anxiety and uncertainty about what was most important and whose demands should be met first. The root of her problem was confusion resulting from a failure to set daily, weekly, and monthly priorities at work. So Ally focused on establishing an orderly set of priorities on the job. This way, she was better able to concentrate on one item of business at a time—and her productivity increased markedly.

Change #3: Your powers of concentration will improve.

Many times, it's necessary to deal not only with very broad priorities in your life—such as those relating to God, family, and country—but also with more limited concerns, such as whether or not to turn on the TV. In this regard, we've noticed that many people are tempted to exercise "bifocal" or "trifocal" vision when making use of their time. That is, they try to do two or three things at once, rather than centering on one concern at a time.

Of course, there's nothing wrong with doing several things at once on some occasions—such as using a multiple or polyphasic approach to several light pastimes as a means to relax. But such split activity can be absolutely deadly to efficiency if you are really trying to accomplish something worthwhile. You simply won't be able to concentrate well, and that means that what should take one hour to finish may well take two, three, or four.

A case in point: a college professor often took about one hour's worth of work home from the office. To make his efforts more palatable, he would turn on the television as he tried to work. Usually he got started right after dinner, at about 8:30 P.M. But he found that he was regularly sitting up until 1:00 or 2:00 A.M. finishing his tasks. In other words, he was spending more than three hours doing one hour's work! Furthermore, this TV-work combination left him no time for high-quality interactions with his two children or his wife.

The professor knew that while he was at home, his primary priority should be his family. He had made that conscious commitment years before, and as inconsistent as he may have been, he still believed in the importance of this principle. So the first thing he did was resolve to devote the early hours of the evening to his wife and children, allowing no distractions from TV or work. Second, he took steps to *separate* his TV from his work. At about 10:00 P.M., he set aside some time to focus *only* on his work and kept the TV off for the one hour he assigned to that task. That left half an hour to an hour for watching television before bed.

This way, he was able to retire by midnight instead of an hour or two later. Even more important, his priorities involving his family were able to be placed in proper order. So paying close attention to priorities gave this man a vehicle for greatly enhancing his powers of concentration on each of the things that was most important in his life.

Change #4: Your time will assume ultimate significance.

A focus on priorities marks the beginning of a successful search for the four-hour day—and for the kind of time control that you want in your life. Once you settle on your major and minor priorities and begin to organize your life so as to realize those priorities, you'll experience the greatest benefit of all: a deep and satisfying sense that your life has more of a definite direction and an ultimate meaning. You'll feel that you are *investing* your time rather than spending it. Instead of feeling that you're running around in circles, or heading nowhere, or constantly operating at loose ends, you'll most likely perceive a broader plan for your existence.

We're not going to take the final step and tell you what to believe or what priorities you should affirm. That's for you to decide. But if you hope to make superior use of your time, you *must* start by exploring your values and then making a commitment to some specific beliefs about what is most important in your life. Otherwise, achieving the four-hour day, or any other satisfying personal time objective, will be impossible. But how exactly do you go about determining your priorities?

HOW TO DETERMINE YOUR PERSONAL PRIORITIES

To determine your overriding priorities in life, you may find one or more of the following exercises helpful. The first involves writing your own obituary. The second includes listing and ranking the basic values that you hold dear. And the third focuses on sorting through the conflicting values that bombard you from the outside world—especially those from your workplace.

Write your own obituary. Strange as it may sound, researchers in matters related to death and dying have found that one of the best ways to assess the meaning of your life, as well as to settle on your main priorities, is to imagine yourself, *after* your death, writing your own obituary.

Unlike the typical obituary that goes into a newspaper, however, this write-up should go beyond a mere description of what you've accomplished in your career. It should also focus on the significance of who you are *inside*; on personal strengths and special traits; on the quality of the relationships you've created; and on the contributions you've made to other individuals and to society. You're *not* limited in this exercise to what you've actually accomplished or become at this point. The idea is to project ahead and consider what you'd *like* to become and how you'd *like* to be remembered. Most likely you'll discover that your most deeply held values will emerge (perhaps including some that you haven't thought about for years!). At this point, don't worry about the order in which you list these achievements or qualities. Just jot them down as they occur to you.

Now, after you've written a first draft, rewrite your obituary with the qualities, achievements, and personal characteristics listed in descending order of importance or priority. When you're finished, you will have a very helpful word picture of what the personal priorities in your life should be.

List and rank your personal values. This exercise is a variation on writing your own obituary, but you may want to try both just to be sure you didn't leave something important out. Also, this particular listing-and-ranking approach can take you one step further by emphasizing *taking action* to realize or fulfill your stated priorities. Again, you'll need a separate sheet of paper.

STEP #1.   List ten of your most important values, guiding principles for living, or highest life priorities. Put them down in any order that comes to mind. These may include family, prestige, honesty, wealth, knowing God, serving the poor, or anything else you feel is important. Feel free to refer back to the things you mentioned in your obituary, and include them here.

STEP #2.   Rewrite the above priorities, with the items listed in order of their importance to you, beginning with the most important and ending with the least important.

STEP #3.   Finally, write out each of your priorities as an action. For example, if you listed "family" as one of your values in Step #2, you might now write, "Care for my family members by giving time and energy to them." Or if you gave a priority to "prestige," you might expand that by saying, "Build personal prestige by gaining awards." Or "honesty" might become "Be honest in all my dealings, both in business and private life."

List the six main priorities of your supervisor, company, or career. Work and career priorities often clash with personal priorities. To be able to reconcile these conflicts, it's essential to put *all* the priorities in your life on the table at the very beginning. So ask yourself these questions:

- What are the most important values or objectives that your supervisor affirms and which he or she wants to impose on you?

- What are the most important values or objectives of your company—especially those that have a direct impact on your own work?

- What is the ultimate destination of the career you've chosen?

We suggest listing six priorities with the idea that you might want to list two for each of the above categories. But it may be that you just want to focus on your supervisor. Or if you're the head of your company, you may want to concentrate only on the company. Or if you're an independent professional, your main interest may be in your career direction.

A priority of your supervisor may be to get the best possible work out of you, regardless of how many hours you have to spend on the job. Or maybe the supervisor, at some level, really does have your overall interests at heart and desires to see you develop a healthy balance between family and work. In part, he may feel that this balance will make you happier and more productive on the job.

As for company values, a major priority is usually to maximize profits. There may also be goals of developing team relationships on the job, producing the highest-quality merchandise in the business, or serving customers so well that loyal, repeat buyers become the norm.

Your ultimate career target may include being promoted all the way up to chief executive officer; or acquiring the reputation of being the best bankruptcy lawyer in your city; or being recognized as the most concerned health care specialist among your peers.

Reconcile your personal priorities with outside priorities. The time has arrived to fine-tune the priorities in your life. Obviously, if your personal priorities conflict with external demands, such as those at work, you'll find yourself in a fragmented, stressful situation. You'll be pulled in one direction by forces in the workplace that expect one type of action or beliefs from you, and in an entirely different direction by your personal convictions.

The negative personal results could range from being immobilized, to confusion, to high anxiety and guilt. You'll be so preoccupied with resolving these conflicts that you'll find you're operating with extreme inefficiency—and wasting prodigious amounts of time. So it's necessary, somehow, to mesh or reconcile these different sets of values. Here's one way to do it:

- First, write down the conflicts or problems you face in integrating your personal values with those posed by your job. For example, you may have as a personal priority "to build my self-esteem," and your company may have as a priority "to promote good customer service." But you find you often run into customers who try to damage your self-esteem.

- Second, explore possible solutions to reconciling conflicting personal and outside priorities. With the above self-esteem illustration, you might find that you can actually strengthen your self-esteem and self-confidence by learning to deal with difficult or obnoxious customers. Among other things, you may decide you need to consult a supervisor or more seasoned worker who has acquired the ability to deal with difficult people. After that, you may be able to apply some of that person's knowledge and experience to your situation.

It's absolutely essential that you formulate a consistent set of overall priorities involving both your personal and work life. It's also essential that you live in a way that's consistent or congruent with those priorities. Any conflict between priorities, or between your actions and your priorities, will cause stress, inefficiency, fatigue, a lack of productivity—and a waste of time.

But once you've put your priorities in order and begun to live consistently with them, you'll find your use of time improves dramatically. It's only after you've sorted through your basic values and objectives, as we've suggested in this chapter, that you'll be ready to consider designing your personal four-hour day.

Chapter Four

Designing Your Personal Four-Hour Day

It's time to dream a little. Prepare to let your imagination soar. Your assignment now is to conceive of what a *series of perfect days* in your life might look like. Don't let any restrictions or qualifications limit your fantasies. Here are a few examples that have been suggested to us by others:

- A physician said she would like to move to a Caribbean island, provide medical services to poor people for three or four hours a day, and spend the rest of her time on the beach.

- A corporate executive said he would like to retire early and spend most of his time with his wife and three children, who, he feels, have not received enough attention from him.

- A schoolteacher would like to put in fewer hours so that he could have time to work on a book he has been longing to write.

- A public relations representative would like to start her own business, a move that she feels would allow her flexible hours and more time to spend with her children.

Now take a few moments to fantasize about how, in the best of all possible worlds, you'd like to use *your* time. Write these fantasies down on a sheet of paper so that you can refer back to them later.

★★★★

Fantasy, of course, must always be tempered by reality, at least where one's daily schedule is concerned. There are usually a number of necessary conditions that must be met, such as earning money, nurturing a family, and meeting various other obligations. Still, it's often helpful to begin formulating your design for a four-hour day in the realm of fantasy, as you've just done. With your imagination free to roam about, you're likely to take into consideration all those factors that will make you happy and satisfied, even if you must qualify and adjust them later to meet the demands of real life.

Now, with your wildest fantasies written out before you on the table, let's begin to shape them into a realistic, workable format. Your next assignment is to design an actual four-hour day *work* schedule that you just might be able to implement in your daily life.

DESIGNING A REAL-LIFE FOUR-HOUR DAY

Your goal here is to design a day that (1) includes four hours of work *and* (2) contains activities or appointments that support your basic priorities in life. To some extent, we're still in the realm of fantasy here. For one thing, your notes outlining your imagined perfect day should remind you to consider everything that you think may contribute to your ultimate personal fulfillment. We're also still in fantasyland at this point because you don't have to worry yet about getting your boss to approve this particular schedule. That's a challenge that comes later, after you've fine-tuned your proposed four-hour day still further.

But we *are* moving closer to reality in several ways. For one thing, you may not have included any work time at all in the previous exercise. Now, you'll have to insert at least four hours a day of gainful employment (or more, if your ideal day involves more work). Also, you'll be asked to take into account all your important life priorities, which you listed and pondered in the previous chapter. As you prepare this initial design for your four-hour workday, keep these principles in mind:

Principle #1: Build in four hours of work or work-related activity each day.

When most people begin to project a series of "perfect" days indefinitely into the future, they almost always incorporate some sort of work into the scenario. Even those who contemplate retirement will often include some regular form of worklike volunteer activity, such as providing services to needy people in their community. There is a time-honored assumption that unless you're rather old, you'll tend to become bored or dissatisfied without having something interesting and productive to occupy your time—and that "something" frequently includes a form of work. On the other hand, very few people seem to want to work twelve- or fourteen-hour days. Even the standard eight-hour day isn't particularly attractive. For many, about four to six hours seems the ideal. That amount is just long enough to accomplish something worthwhile, but not so long as to tire you out or make the day seem as if it's devoted entirely to labor. Of course, it's up to you to determine the *type* of work you'd like to do.

Principle #2: Incorporate your personal priorities into your perfect day.

Refer back to the priorities you established for yourself in the previous chapter. There, you identified both non-work and work priorities, and you made an effort to reconcile your company's or supervisor's priorities with your own. These priorities *must* be reflected in your ideal schedule. If they are not, you'll experience a sense of incongruence, fragmentation, or inconsistency. You'll be in danger of feeling as though you're being pulled in different directions. The resulting internal conflicts will make you less content, productive, and efficient. In such a state of turmoil, the benefits of the four-hour day will disappear.

How do you incorporate your personal priorities into your ideal day? Consider the approach taken by Geri, a single mother who worked as a creative director for a major advertising firm. Geri had become frustrated with her job because she found herself working nine or ten hours a day at the office—and at the same time having to supervise care for her children. She felt torn between her children and her need to support them. Geri's main problem was that she had a set of personal priorities that had not been incorporated successfully into her daily life. When she was asked to list her major priorities, both outside and inside her career, in descending order of importance, she came up with this:

1. MY CHILDREN:	I want to be at home when my son arrives home from school or sports, and I want to be available to help him with his homework or just listen to his problems and concerns. And I want to spend a few hours each day with my daughter in the playground or on playdates with neighborhood kids.
2. MY WORK:	I want to be in a challenging job so that I can further my career and professional expertise as much as possible. Also, I want to make enough money to cover the basic needs of my family; to provide a

vacation trip each year; to save a little for their college education; and, if possible, to contribute to my own pension fund.

3. MY WOMEN FRIENDS: I want to stay in regular contact with my three or four best friends. That means seeing each of them, either together or alone, at least twice a month.

4. DATING: I want to be available to go out on a date about once a week.

These may sound like modest objectives—unless you're a conscientious single parent. Juggling the demands of career, family, and friends is a hard enough chore for a two-parent family, but when there's only *one* parent, the time squeeze can become excruciating.

Geri decided that in her ideal day, she would work four to five hours, from 11:00 A.M. to 12:30 P.M., and from about 1:30 to about 4:30 P.M. This way, she could spend time with her three-year-old in the morning; help her son get off to school; interact with her three-year-old again at lunchtime; and be available for her son when he arrived home from school in the afternoon. She also planned on being home every school night, Sunday through Thursday. In this way, she could have dinner with her children and if necessary, be available to help her son with his homework.

This plan took care of her first two priorities, her family and her career. But what about the other two, her women friends and dating? These final two priorities were absolutely essential for Geri to feel she was leading a full life, but they also had the potential to increase her time pressures significantly. In fact, if she continued to work eight or nine hours a day, she knew she would be overwhelmed by the demands she was placing on herself.

The answer to her dilemma seemed to lie in sticking unwaveringly to a working day of four to five hours. If she achieved that objective, she knew she could schedule at least one non-school evening for a date on the weekends. Also, she would have the flexibility to build in periodic lunches or other get-togethers with her friends. She even found that she would actually have some extra time that she could devote to her family or to volunteer activities, if she so chose. With Geri, as with many other people who are feeling heavy scheduling pressures, the four-hour workday appeared to be the key to incorporating personal priorities successfully into daily life. (Exactly *how* a person like Geri can achieve these ambitious goals is the subject of later chapters.)

Principle #3: Once you've arrived at an ideal schedule for your personal four-hour day, write it down.

It will be helpful to buy a notebook, a journal, or some other booklet with blank pages to record your reflections and plans on your use of time. At this point, you should write down a tentative schedule for your four-hour day, with specific times indicated for fulfilling the priorities you've identified.

As we've mentioned, at this stage you needn't worry about how you're actually going to implement this four-hour day. Dealing with supervisors, clients, and ethical problems related to your use of time on the job involves issues we'll deal with in another context. All you need right now is a snapshot of what you want your perfect four-hour day to look like. That gives you a goal to shoot for, an ideal agenda you will most likely have to adjust somewhat in the face of the demands of the marketplace. Your final, real-life schedule will emerge after you've moved through the upcoming exercises of analyzing your personal use of time and then formulating a specific time budget.

Chapter Five

Where Do Those Minutes and Hours Go?

Achieving some version of a four-hour workday *is* a realistic possibility for most people. But as we're beginning to see, actually reaching this goal requires you to design and follow carefully a systematic, well-thought-out strategy.

After all, what we're talking about here is an approach to work and leisure that is revolutionary. When you succeed with this program, you'll probably be the only person you know who works only four hours a day—and who thoroughly enjoys those remaining waking hours.

So far, these steps have moved you ever closer to realizing the four-hour day:

- You've begun to open your mind to a new understanding of time, which suggests that the concept of time isn't necessarily fixed or immutable. To some degree you possess the power to speed up or slow down the pace of events and activities in your life.

- You've identified the major priorities in your life and observed that organizing your life according to those priorities is a prerequisite to greater productivity and efficiency.

38

- Keeping your priorities in mind, you've actually produced a preliminary design of your own ideal four-hour day.

Now, the time has arrived for you to begin to settle on a final, practical version of your four-hour day. To this end, you'll have to establish a definite daily schedule—based on what we call a "time budget," which will indicate exactly how you plan to spend your days, hours, and minutes each week.

SPENDING YOUR TIME IS LIKE SPENDING YOUR MONEY

Before you draft your time budget—which involves a step-by-step procedure that we'll discuss in the following chapter—it's necessary first for you to do a time analysis of your typical week. The objective is to find out *precisely* where your time is going. You *must* understand how you're actually using your time, right now, in your everyday life, before you can set up a four-hour-day schedule that will work for you in the future.

Getting started with time analysis. Much as you might do in drawing up a financial budget, you should now begin to draft a set of raw time-use notes that indicate what you do *every minute* of the day—for one week. This means recording *every* activity during that week, no matter how insignificant it may seem. In making these notes, begin at the time you rise in the morning and continue to the moment that you go to bed at night. You have to know where the time is *actually* going before you try to determine where it *should* be going.

THE NUTS AND BOLTS OF PERSONAL TIME ANALYSIS

A detailed, nuts-and-bolts approach to analyzing your current use of time will take an entire seven-day period; this will ensure you've included all your time-use activities. Here are some points to keep in mind as you proceed with your analysis:

- Remember there are 168 hours in one week. The objective in doing a personal time analysis is to know what you're doing during each of those hours.

- Record fractions of hours. If you start a meeting ten minutes late and finish five minutes early, indicate that in your notes.

- Sleep time should be recorded from the time you lie down in bed and turn out the lights—not from the time you think you actually drift off into dreamland. On the other hand, if you read or talk in bed, those activities should not be included as sleep.

- Set up as many different categories of time use as you need. Detailing these segments now can be helpful as you try to cut out wasted minutes and hours later.

- Don't forget "dead time," preparation time, or transition time between activities. These periods may include waiting for an appointment to begin; commuting to work; traveling between appointments; getting dressed; or ordinary grooming, such as shaving, washing your face, and brushing your teeth in the morning.

- Include meals, snacks, casual conversation at the watercooler, and telephone conversations.

- Time spent reading magazines and newspapers must also be noted.

After you've gone through this time-analysis exercise, you'll most likely be amazed to see where your minutes and hours are going each week. Steve, an insurance salesman, certainly was, and his analysis provided him with an extremely valuable foundation for reordering his life to achieve a four-hour day.

> **Warning:** The following analysis and calculations do get rather complex at points, but stay with the illustration. You'll find that when you start doing your own time analysis, it will be tempting to explore even more variations than what we've included here for Steve.

STEVE'S AMAZING TIME ADVENTURE

Although he didn't think he was doing much more than anyone else he knew, Steve felt under constant time pressure. His insurance business, which he had been pursuing for about fifteen years, was going well. Still, Steve's typical day was packed with meetings, phone calls, and paperwork. He arrived at his office by 8:00 A.M., and he rarely returned home before 7:00 P.M.

When he finally walked through the front door, his wife, who also held down a full-time job, had usually started putting together the family meal—which Steve helped prepare as soon as he put down his briefcase and took off his suit coat. After the family meal was finished, Steve pitched in to help one or more of their three children with their homework or otherwise interact with them. (On weekends, he also always tried to attend their important athletic events or other activities.) By 11:00 P.M., the children were finally in bed, and Steve and his wife sat down to talk, watch TV, or read for about an hour before heading for bed.

On top of these activities, Steve was also deeply involved in three nonprofit, charitable activities: a teaching assignment at his church; board membership for a local musical group; and volunteering for a service organization

that provided tutoring services for poor children. Steve
was always feeling pressed for time, and he frequently felt
quite guilty when he had to turn down requests from one
of his charity contacts to help out in some additional way.
He almost never balked at giving money; his problem was
that he could see no way to give up any more of his time.
These time pressures, which were becoming increasingly
confusing, upsetting, and tiring, finally caused him to sit
down and do a personal time analysis.

First, he reflected on the major priorities in his life. He
decided that his family came first; his career responsibilities second; and his nonprofit service activities third. Other responsibilities and activities might have some importance, but they
always followed these three in his hierarchy of personal
priorities.

Then he began to keep track of his actual use of time.
After about three days of taking notes, here's an outline
of what Steve learned about his typical week. Note the
precision with which he made his entries.

Sleep:	47.25 hours
Eating:	12.25 hours
Newspaper and magazine reading:	10.5 hours
Television watching:	12.25 hours
Interaction with children:	14.75 hours
Interaction with wife:	8.25 hours
Charitable activities:	3.1 hours
Church work/attendance:	10 hours
Volunteer tutoring:	2 hours
Insurance work:	45 hours
Commuting to work:	5.9 hours
Commuting to volunteer or social activities:	2.7 hours
Personal preparation/grooming time:	6.3 hours
Preparation time preceding family activities:	1.2 hours

Exercise:	4.9 hours
"Dead" or transition time (such as waiting for late clients or arriving at a meeting early):	2.4 hours
Errands/personal business:	4.75 hours

If you get out your calculator and add up these entries, you'll immediately see that Steve had a major problem. His total number of hours came to 193.5—about twenty-five hours more than the total of 168 hours in a week!

Did he make a mistake in recording his time use? He may have been off by a few hours one way or the other. But the main reason he ended up with so many extra hours was that there was some overlap in his calculations. For example, his wife was present for about four of the hours that he spent each week with his children. Also, being a highly efficient person who couldn't stand just to sit around, he made good use of virtually all of his "dead" time and his commuting time (on the train) by reading magazines, newspapers, or other literature—a practice that accounted for more than seven of his reading hours. He also remembered that much of his "eating time" at home—about six hours' worth—overlapped with interactions with his wife and children. So he subtracted the twice-counted times (about seventeen hours) and eliminated mistaken entries (about three hours). In this way, Steve was able to account almost exactly for the 168 hours in his typical week.

But that certainly didn't solve his problems. He did a couple of quick additional calculations and discovered that his weekly nonprofit work—including service on the charitable board, at church, and in volunteer tutoring—added up to 15.1 hours per week. Multiplying that number by 52 (the number of weeks in a year), he saw that he was devoting 785.2 hours per year to these activities. Then came the real shocker: when he divided that 785.2 figure by 8, which in his mind represented the standard eight-hour workday, he discovered that he was devoting 98.15 workdays per year to nonprofit activities! That represented more than one quarter of the eight-hour working days in his year. Obviously Steve wasn't substituting all this nonprofit time for his regular work time. He was doing his nonprofit work *after* his regular work hours. In effect, he was holding down one paying job and one part-time nonprofit job.

In hours and days, here's a comparison between Steve's professional work and his nonprofit commitments: with an average work week of 45 hours, he was spending about 2,205 hours on the job per year (this figure includes 49 weeks of work, as he managed to take off about three weeks a year for vacation and holidays). Those 2,205 hours can also be expressed as 275 standard eight-hour working days a year at his job (2,205 divided by 8). If you add the 98.15 nonprofit eight-hour days per year to this figure, you find that Steve was spending nearly 374 eight-hour days a year just on his career and his nonprofit responsibilities. That's nine days more than the 365 days in a regular year! (*Note:* If you're confused about how Steve could be working at his job *and* doing nonprofit activities for a total of 374 days a year, remember this: we're talking about standard eight-hour workdays here, *not* twenty-four-hour days.)

No matter how you evaluate Steve's situation, it's evident that the burden on him from just these two activities—his career and his nonprofit commitments—was already quite onerous. In effect, as a result of these two activities, he wasn't getting any full days off during the year. He had, in a sense, placed himself in a *negative* time mode, where he was actually working overtime during his leisure hours to cover all his eight-hour-day work and nonprofit commitments. It became clear to him that he should try to cut back on some of his involvements in order to depressurize his life.

Steve's next step was to set up a time budget that incorporated both what he had learned from his time analysis and also the time goals he wanted to achieve in the future. But before we examine Steve's Time Budget, you should first do your own personal time analysis.

DOING YOUR OWN TIME ANALYSIS

Here are some step-by-step guidelines, which are based on what you've already learned about the time analysis procedure.

STEP #1: Keep track of your actual use of time, in hours and minutes, for the next week. If you can estimate precisely where your moments go by spending only a couple of days at this exercise, that's fine. If you need the full week to be sure you catch everything, it's advisable to take the necessary time at this point.

STEP #2: When you've finished recording your time use, crunch some numbers. You'll want to add up the total number of hours you've recorded. Probably, you'll find as Steve did that you've included more than 168 hours in your week. If so, identify those activities that overlap with other activities, and try to find any mistakes you may have made. Also, you should highlight activities that are taking more time than you thought. If you're feeling any particular time pressures, try to isolate the activity or activities that seem to be causing the stress.

STEP #3: See how well your actual use of time reinforces your life priorities, which you identified in Chapter 3. Most likely, you'll find a correlation between the stresses you identified in Step #2 and the lack of agreement between your priorities and time use in this step.

Now, with your personal time analysis in hand, you're ready to start building a time budget, which will be invaluable in helping you revolutionize your life with the four-hour day.

Chapter Six

The Time Budget

A *time analysis*, which you did in the previous chapter, tells you how your hours are now being used. A *time budget*, which you're about to draw up, will show you how your hours *should* be used—and how the four-hour day can be scheduled into your life.

WHAT IS A TIME BUDGET?

Just as a financial budget shows you how you plan to spend your money, a *time budget* is a projection of how you've decided to spend your time. We don't know anyone who has followed a personal financial budget perfectly; there are always mistakes, always pressures that cause more to be spent in one category, or less saved in another. The same observations apply to a time budget. Inevitably, in practice you'll end up spending more or less time than you planned. Still, it's important to have a budget as an ultimate, best-of-all-possible-worlds goal, even if you don't always live up to your expectations. That way, you'll be well on your way to exerting more control over your time and your life.

It will be helpful to keep several guidelines in mind as you draft your time budget:

Reduce your workday to four hours. At this point, don't worry about how you'll actually decrease your working time by this much and still do all you need to do every day. Later, you may decide you actually *want* to devote five or even six hours to your work. Right now, however, all you should focus on is setting up the budget, with a four-hour day as part of the program.

Locate your four-hour day within those hours when you tend to be most efficient. For example, if you work best in the early morning hours, schedule your four hours before lunch. If you are an afternoon person, place your working hours at a later point in the day, just before you leave for home.

Reevaluate your allocation of leisure time. This is a good opportunity to eliminate or compress hours devoted to activities or commitments that you consider marginal in terms of your life priorities. For example, if you're spending time on some fund-raising efforts for a community theater even though your commitment to the theater has waned, maybe you should drop this activity altogether. On the other hand, you may feel you should be spending *more* non-work time in a certain way, such as interacting with your family. If that's the case, by all means increase the hours you allocate to this priority.

Record all your activities for every hour and minute you spend during your typical week. To make this task easier, use the following time budget format:

MODEL TIME BUDGET FORMAT

PERSONAL PRIORITIES:

1.
2.
3.
4.
5.
6.

DAY: _____

HOUR:

6:00 A.M.
7:00
8:00
9:00
10:00
11:00
Noon
1:00 P.M.
2:00
3:00
4:00
5:00
6:00
7:00
8:00
9:00
10:00
11:00

Midnight

1:00 A.M.

2:00

3:00

4:00

5:00

Note: This format should be used to budget each of the seven days in the week.

Before you try to enter your own daily schedule into this scheme, here are some points to keep in mind:

Don't feel tied down to the hourly times indicated on the format. You'll undoubtedly discover that some of your activities and responsibilities begin on the half-hour, on the quarter-hour, or at some other odd time. You should shape your time budget format to accommodate these peculiarities. So if you normally rise at 6:30 A.M., and if you always go out to lunch at 12:45 P.M., indicate those times on your personal budget format.

If one daily format fits several days in your typical week, use one sheet for all the relevant days. As you'll see in the following illustration, Steve's schedules on Tuesday, Wednesday, and Thursday were the same. Consequently, Steve used one Tuesday–Thursday sheet.

Always keep your focus on achieving the top life priorities you've listed. The main purpose of this time budget is *not* just to list the details of your daily schedule. Rather, the primary objective is to arrange your day in such a way that you are much more likely to devote time to reach those goals that you've decided are most important.

To understand exactly how to *use* this budget concept, it will be helpful to consider a practical application of the format. The following is an example of how Steve, the insurance agent described in the previous chapter, employed his time analysis to put together a time budget.

STEVE'S TIME BUDGET

Using his top six life priorities as guiding principles, and resolving to schedule only four to five hours of work each day, Steve came up with a *time budget* that looked like this:

PERSONAL PRIORITIES:

1. Wife
2. Children
3. Work/career
4. Church teaching
5. Charitable board (musical group)
6. Tutoring

DAY: MONDAY

HOUR:

6:00 A.M.	Wake up.
7:45	Finish exercise/wash-up/grooming/dressing/breakfast. Begin commute.
8:30	Finish commute/arrive at office. Read newspaper/transition to work.
9:00	Work.

10:00	Continue work. Include two 15-minute breaks.
11:30	Finish first two hours of work. Begin research on Sunday school lesson.
12:30 P.M.	Finish Sunday school lesson. Go to lunch.
1:00	Continue lunch.
2:00	Do personal business (banking/bills/errands) for 45 minutes. Return to office. On the phone with wife for 15 minutes.
3:00	Begin work, including client contacts.
4:00	Continue work.
5:00	Finish work (2 hours). Begin commute.
6:00	Finish commute. Transition to supper (15 minutes). Begin supper with family.
7:00	Finish supper. Prepare for tutorial.
7:30	Begin tutorial of needy child.
9:00	Be available to help children with homework.
9:30	Begin reading newspaper or other periodicals or personal matter.
10:00	Finish reading. Watch some TV. Spend time with wife.
11:00	To bed.
Midnight	
1:00 A.M.	
2:00	
3:00	

4:00
5:00

DAY: TUESDAY–THURSDAY

HOUR:

6:00 A.M.   Wake up

7:45   Finish exercise/wash-up/grooming/
            dressing/breakfast. Begin
            commute.

8:30   Finish commute/arrive at office. Read
            paper/transition to work.

9:00   Work.

10:00   Continue work. Include two 15-
            minute breaks.

11:30   Finish first two hours of work. Begin
            research on Sunday school lesson.

12:30 P.M. Finish Sunday school lesson. Go to
            lunch with client.

1:00   Continue lunch (total of one hour in
            discussion with client).

2:00   Do personal business (banking/bills/
            errands) for 45 minutes. Return
            from lunch. On the phone with wife
            for 15 minutes.

3:00   Begin work, including client contacts.

4:00   Continue work.

5:00   Finish work (2 hours). Begin
            commute.

6:00   Finish commute. Transition to supper
            (15 minutes). Begin supper with
            family.

7:00	Finish supper. Be available to help children with homework.
9:30	Begin reading newspaper or other periodicals or personal matter.
10:00	Finish reading. Watch some TV. Spend time with wife.
11:00	To bed.
Midnight	
1:00 A.M.	
2:00	
3:00	
4:00	
5:00	

DAY: FRIDAY

HOUR:

6:00 A.M.	Wake up.
7:45	Finish exercise/wash-up/grooming/ dressing/breakfast. Begin commute.
8:30	Finish commute/arrive at office. Read paper/transition to work.
9:00	Work.
10:00	Continue work. Include two 15-minute breaks.
11:30	Finish first two hours of work. Begin work on music board issues.
12:30 P.M.	Finish music board work. Go to lunch.
1:00	Continue lunch.
2:00	Do personal business (banking/bills/

errands) for 45 minutes. Return to office. On phone with wife for 15 minutes.

3:00	Begin work, including client contacts.
4:00	Continue work.
5:00	Finish work (2 hours). Begin commute.
6:00	Finish commute. Transition to supper (15 minutes). Begin supper with family.
7:00	Finish supper. Prepare for regular weekly "date" with wife.
7:30	Go out with wife.
11:00	Arrive back home.
11:30	To bed.
Midnight	
1:00 A.M.	
2:00	
3:00	
4:00	
5:00	

DAY: SATURDAY

HOUR:

7:45 A.M.	Wake up/exercise/wash-up/grooming/dress.
9:00	Breakfast with family.
10:00	Finish breakfast. Begin to prepare for kids' sports events (or family outing, when there are no athletics).

3:00 P.M.	Return from sports events. Begin errands or shopping.
4:00	Return home after errands or shopping. Begin Sunday school lesson preparation.
6:00	Finish Sunday school lesson preparation. Enter transition time before supper with family.
6:30	Supper with family begins.
7:30	Finish supper. Relax, read, watch TV.
9:30	Begin reading newspaper or other periodicals or personal matter. Family interactions.
11:30	To bed.
Midnight	
1:00 A.M.	
2:00	
3:00	
4:00	
5:00	

DAY: SUNDAY

HOUR:

7:45 A.M.	Wake up/exercise/wash-up/grooming/dress.
9:00	Breakfast.
9:30	Commute to church.
9:45	Begin to teach Sunday school lesson.
10:45	Finish lesson. Church and coffee hour.
1:00 P.M.	Finish coffee hour. Commute home.

1:30	Lunch. Relax, read Sunday paper, watch TV. Time with family.
3:30	Commute to music board meeting or related committee meeting.
4:00	Music board or committee meeting.
6:00	Finish music board or committee meeting. Commute home.
6:30	Supper with family begins.
7:30	Finish supper. Relax, read, watch TV.
8:00	Be available to help with kids' homework. Family interactions.
9:30	Read paper, watch TV. Time with wife.
11:00	To bed.
Midnight	
1:00 A.M.	
2:00	
3:00	
4:00	
5:00	

AN EVALUATION OF STEVE'S TIME BUDGET

What kind of job did Steve do in drafting his time budget? Remember: his main goal was to set up his week so that he would be able to work more effectively toward his stated life priorities. Here are the results.

PRIORITY #1:   His budget enabled him to increase the time he spent with his wife from 8.5 to 9 hours per week.

PRIORITY #2:   His budget provided the opportunity to spend 15.25 hours a week with his children, instead of the 14.75 hours he had been spending (according to his previous time analysis).

PRIORITY #3: Steve's budget incorporated a workday that varied between four and five hours, in contrast to the nine hours per day he had been working.

Of course, when Steve drew up the time budget, he didn't know exactly how he would achieve a four-hour day. A number of questions were still in his mind: How will I get everything done that I need to accomplish in such a short period of time? How will it look to my colleagues if I seem to be working much shorter hours than anyone else? If Steve had been working for a boss, he might also have asked: How can I possibly convince my supervisor that I'm pulling my load at work on four to five hours a day? The knowledge and insights necessary to respond to these questions would come later for Steve, as he implemented some of the concepts that will be discussed in some detail in Chapters 7 through 11.

PRIORITY #4: His time budget enabled Steve to increase the time he spent each week on his church work and attendance from 10 hours to 11.25 hours.

PRIORITY #5: He continued to spend about the same amount of time, three hours, on the charitable board work with the music group.

PRIORITY #6: He also devoted about the same amount of time as he had previously to tutoring a needy youngster—two hours per week.

As you can see, the time budget provided a means—on

paper, at least—for Steve to do a better job of achieving the life priorities he had established for himself. In addition, he managed to make headway toward realizing some secondary objectives: he cut his television time from 12.25 hours a week to 6 hours. And he also increased his sleep time from 47.25 hours a week, an amount he had considered too little for optimum health, to 51.25 hours.

But how can Steve—or you, when you set up your own weekly schedule—ensure that a time budget will *really work*? How can you be reasonably sure that you'll be able to incorporate a four-hour workday into your life, improve your ability to accomplish your life priorities, *and* make the best use of the non-work time that this limited amount of work sets free?

A fundamental first step in making the transition from a budget on paper to a budget that lives and breathes in the real world is to make sure your time budget fits into what we call your "rhythm of life."

Chapter Seven

Using Your Rhythm of Life

Time-management systems and self-help books don't work. At least, they fail miserably in enabling anyone to achieve a *permanent* transformation of personal time—a transformation that can make possible the incorporation of a four-hour workday into your schedule.

Certainly, learning some strategic time-management tips—such as ways to reduce procrastination, eliminate unnecessary paperwork, and streamline personal organization—can help you save time and increase productivity, at least for a while. But usually, these techniques are just Band-Aid treatments that temporarily mask more serious, deep-rooted problems. The problem with most time-management programs is that they don't provide ways to enable well-meaning students to follow through and change their lives. What's missing is a way to identify one's *life priorities* and establish ways to fulfill those priorities. The secret to experiencing a "time revolution" in your life—including the fulfillment of your personal priorities—is first to understand exactly what your *rhythm of life* is. Then you'll be ready to fit your daily activities into the flow of that rhythm.

WHAT'S YOUR RHYTHM OF LIFE?

Your *rhythm of life* may be understood as a combination of four factors that make you "run well" as a person:

1. Your personal priorities
2. Your most efficient times during the day
3. The particular work or activity that gives you the most enjoyment
4. The atmosphere, including the physical environment and people, in which you put out your best efforts

Some of us *naturally* move more slowly or quickly or energetically than others at different times of the day. Some affirm one set of beliefs about what's moral or immoral, true or false; others are just as committed to a different, perhaps diametrically opposed set of beliefs—and their choices about what to do in their daily lives reflect those beliefs.

Serious problems with personal time use arise when you try to arrange your schedule or do things that are out of sync with the track—or *rhythm of life*—on which you operate best. So if you try to do your most important work in the morning, even though you're an "afternoon person," you'll be less efficient. If you slip into actions that are inconsistent with your basic beliefs about right and wrong, you'll experience serious stress, fatigue, anxiety, and inefficiency. And if you allow your daily schedule to get out of control, so that you're not taking any steps to further your life priorities, you'll experience deep dissatisfaction—and a sense that your time isn't counting for much.

The simplest way to determine your rhythm of life is to ask yourself these questions:

WHAT ARE MY TOP LIFE PRIORITIES?

You've already listed these in Chapter Three. Review them now. You may want to rethink or rephrase them, just to be sure that they reflect how you really feel about what's important in your life.

What Times of the Day Do I Work or Think Most Efficiently?

It's essential for you to understand whether you're a "morning person," an "afternoon person," or a "night person." Most likely you work or think quite well at more than one time of the day. In any case, identify the time or times when you are at peak performance and resolve to concentrate your most important activities during those periods.

What Work or Leisure Activities Motivate Me the Most?

Those who *like* what they do tend to be the most creative, effective performers. They tend to make maximum use of their time. On the other hand, those who hate their work or are bored by it will never give it their best or maximize their time.

What Atmosphere, Environment, or People Bring Out the Best in Me?

You may operate best in a quiet, serene, bucolic setting, far from the fast-moving urban hullabaloo. Or you may be stimulated and inspired by a swirl of talk and activity. Most of us don't function well around negative people who are always putting others down. But some do like some disagreement and conflict around them, just to "keep them on their toes." Each of us has different reactions to the physical and emotional atmosphere in the office or home. So spend some time thinking through your preferences, and try to shape or select your environment in a way that will make you happier and more satisfied—and enhance your productivity and efficiency.

Now set aside a few moments to think through how you

would describe your own rhythm of life. Jot down your thoughts so that you can refer back to them later.

★★★★

With this new understanding of your personal *rhythm of life*, you're better prepared to reevaluate the *time budget* you drew up in the previous chapter—and to consider ways to use it as a motivational tool that can help you change your life permanently.

TOWARD A TOTAL TIME REVOLUTION

The problem with the time budget that you formulated is that, like most other self-help devices, it's likely to be filed in a drawer or lost—unless you take steps *right now* to make it a living, breathing, life-transforming force in your everyday existence. What can you do to bring about this personal time revolution? Just follow these three "rules for a time revolution." These will help you merge your time budget, which is now just words on paper, and your rhythm of life, that pace or flow of your daily existence that reflects who you really are.

First Rule for Revolution: Focus consciously, *every day*, on your life priorities.

There are several ways to do this. One that we like is just to write those five or six priorities down on a sheet of paper and insert them into your wallet. Then, at least once a day, pull out the list and meditate on it.

As you reflect, ask yourself, "Who am I—*really*?" Then ask, "Who do I want to become?" Finally, ask, "What do I want out of life?" Your list of priorities should provide you with immediate responses to these questions. If you find that they don't give you an answer, you'll probably want to rethink your priorities and perhaps change them. Or perhaps you'll just need to deepen your understanding of your priorities.

Obviously, defining and understanding your priorities is not always such a simple task! On the other hand, this sort of reflection almost always produces a deeper understanding of who you are and what you want out of life. And the better you understand yourself and organize your life to accommodate that understanding, the better and more enjoyable use you'll make of your time.

Second Rule for Revolution: Don't take the details of your *time budget* too seriously.

What are we saying here!? We've spent pages upon pages—and encouraged you to spend up to a week keeping records—so that you could analyze your use of time and design a *time budget*. And now we're saying don't take it too seriously! What's going on? First, when you embarked on this adventure in time, it was extremely important for you to do a time analysis so that you would know as precisely as possible where every minute was going. The process of time analysis is invaluable in learning how you're using, or misusing, your time—and to find out whether you're sincerely supporting the life priorities you identified, or just paying lip service to them. If you don't know where you're going wrong, you can't very well take corrective action! Second, the exercise of formulating a time budget is just as essential. To use your time wisely and to behave in a way that's consistent with your priorities you have to get into the habit of *planning* your days.

Having said this, however, we must build some realism and flexibility into our scenario. *No one* is going to make out a comprehensive, detailed time budget of the type you've constructed and follow it to the letter for the rest of his or her life. We know and you know that no matter how honorable your intentions, time budgets, like financial budgets, are made to be violated. The main thing you've done in putting it together is give yourself a target. If you hit the target most of the time—or even 50 percent of the time—you'll be a better person for it.

On the other hand, I don't want to suggest that your

time budget is mostly useless or that you should feel free to ignore it whenever you like. The key point to keep in mind with the time budget is this: when you look it over—and you should spend a minute or so each week glancing through it—you should immediately perceive the *big picture* of your life. You should recall what your major life priorities are and how you're working toward achieving them each day. If you see you've been neglecting some item in the budget, you might consider rescheduling that item for a time when you'll be more likely to accomplish it. The time budget shouldn't be a vehicle for fostering extra guilt in your life just because you're not living up to your expectations of yourself. Rather, it's a general plan, a map that can help you keep on a road that will lead you to the final destination you've picked for yourself.

Third Rule for Revolution: Ease into your personal time transformation.

It's not so easy to make the projections and priorities contained in your time budget fit perfectly into your rhythm of life. It takes more time than you might expect to effect the kind of personal transformation, or revolution, we're talking about here. So feel free to move slowly and steadily as you try to mesh your budget with the demands of everyday existence. This gradual, relaxed approach to making your *time budget* work in practice is especially important if you hope eventually to incorporate a four-hour day into your life. So if you find at first that you simply can't cut your working time to four or five hours a day, but that you *can* make it down to six or seven hours, that's fine! Feel free to adjust your time budget to temporarily accommodate these longer working hours.

In practical terms, the way you'll eventually achieve your four-hour day—and a daily schedule that powerfully affirms all your life priorities—is the subject of the remaining chapters in this book. In those sections, you'll learn the nitty-gritty of such topics as:

- Orchestrating your "transition time"
- Breaking through the many "time barriers" in your life, or those obstacles that cause you to waste time
- Developing certain key "speed skills" that will empower you to finish tasks at lightning-fast speed
- Fighting successfully for your four-hour day in environments where the nature of the job or the attitude of the boss is hostile to your objectives.

Now, let's see what you can do to achieve a better understanding of "transition time."

Chapter Eight

Understanding Transition Time

Huge chunks of your days and weeks disappear as anonymous periods that might be called "transition time." These minutes and hours tick away as you're moving from one activity to another, or waiting for the next appointment to begin, or traveling to work or some social activity. Some people call these connecting moments in the day "dead time," because they are often wasted.

Once you've settled on your major life priorities, formulated a time budget based on those priorities, and begun to integrate the budget into your rhythm of life, your next challenge is to learn to make much better use of your transition, or dead, time. Plugging productive career and volunteer efforts into those empty spaces of the day will not only make you more efficient, you'll also be in a much stronger position to fulfill your personal priorities *and* achieve the four-hour workday.

How much time do you spend in transition activities in a typical week? Check your time budget again—especially such items as commuting to work and traveling to volunteer activities; personal preparation and grooming time; preparation time preceding family activities; and other transition time. You may want to compare your results with those of Steve in Chapter 5. His time analysis revealed that before he did his time budget, he spent at least 18.5 hours in transition each week. Actually, when you add in coffee breaks and other such periods, his total transition time went much higher—even after he had streamlined his day with the time budget. Let's suppose that you spend eighteen hours in transition time each week. How can you make better use of those hours? Here are some suggestions:

THE BASIC PRINCIPLES FOR USING YOUR TRANSITION TIME

PRINCIPLE #1: Unnecessary, wasteful activity should be eliminated during transition time.

If for example, you spend an hour just after you get up in the morning in washing up, grooming, dressing, and other preparatory activity, you might try to reduce that time by fifteen minutes, or even a half-hour. This way, you'd gain up to an extra half-hour to use in more productive ways. You might sleep a little longer, or you might spend the saved time planning your day's schedule; you could even include some meditation.

PRINCIPLE #2: It's essential to *do two things at once* during commuting or waiting time.

This approach might also be described as a "doubling up" strategy for transition time. As a general rule, it's dangerous to try to do two or more things at once because this resulting fragmentation of your concentration and attention can make you less efficient. As we've already seen, "bifocal" or "trifocal" involvement in activities—such as television plus work, or television plus leisure reading, or television plus reading plus conversation with family members—will almost always result in lower productivity and an overall waste of time. But with transition, or dead, time, the situation is different. In many transition slots, if you fail to do two things at once (such as combining commuting with productive conversation, or combining waiting for a meeting with reading), you may find you're making relatively poor use of your time.

PRINCIPLE #3: Solitude is often helpful to maximize the use of transition time.

Obviously, it's not always possible to find a place to be alone when you're in transition between one activity and another. On the other hand, if you think creatively, you may find you have more opportunities to isolate yourself than you first realized. For example, if you arrive early for an appointment, you may find yourself alone in a waiting room. Or you might ask if you could use an empty office or conference room. Spending a few minutes by yourself this way can do wonders in helping you make last-minute preparations for a meeting, or in reading some material that you'd otherwise have to spend time with later.

Sometimes it's also helpful to *simulate* solitude by learning to block out the presence of people and activities around you. Many seasoned travelers have discovered ways to go into a state of highly focused concentration when they are on airplanes, trains, or other forms of public transportation. One saleswoman who spends many hours in airplanes says that she is able to erect an "invisible shield" around herself by immediately pulling out business papers when she sits down in her seat. Other passengers invariably respect her privacy when they see her working, and the high seats in front of her help block out distracting movements from her line of vision. She actually finds that she can concentrate more intensely when she's flying than when she's in her office.

So look for ways to build some solitude into your transition time. Any extra hours you can gain on a plane, or extra minutes on a commuting train or bus, will enhance productivity and assist you greatly in finishing work or personal tasks.

PRINCIPLE #4:   It's important to have an explicit plan for your transition time.

Vague intentions won't help you maximize the use of transition periods. A physician who frequently had minutes tucked away between operations or appointments found that he was wasting those precious moments because he had failed to plan their productive use. So he installed in his office a TV monitor that was tuned in to a financial news network that supplied constantly updated market reports. Also, on a table in front of the TV he spread out the stock listings from the current *Wall Street Journal*, as well as stock reports he received from Value Line and Standard & Poor's, and information from other services. As a result of this prior planning, the doctor was able to become involved without delay in his investment concerns when he had a few minutes to himself. He became much better informed about his portfolio and better prepared to make decisions about his investments. In this way, he made highly productive use of what had previously been wasted ''dead'' time.

To what uses might you put your transition periods? There are at least five, several of which have already been mentioned, but which deserve further consideration.

THE BEST USES OF TRANSITION TIME

1. EXTRA READING OR WORK

This is probably the most obvious use of the often-lost moments that are tucked in between meetings or during travel or commuting. Yet so many people fail to employ these scattered periods wisely.

The next time you're in a reception area or waiting room, note how many of the people around you are just sitting there, staring blankly into space; others may be thumbing aimlessly through magazines. Increasing numbers of travelers, however, are learning how valuable the hours spent on airplanes or trains can be—and many have learned to make use of that time. They immediately pull out a sheaf of business papers, a laptop computer, or other materials and turn out some of their highest-quality work. Others pack newspapers, professional journals, books, or other reading that they know they have to do at some point, and they polish it off while waiting or in transit.

The majority of people waste those precious moments—but *you* won't fall into this trap if you think through your day and develop a personal strategy for transition periods. To maximize your use of this connecting time, it's necessary to plan ahead. You should first look over your schedule and identify the transitions, or dead times, when you could be doing extra work or reading. Then, pack the materials you need to accomplish these tasks. Finally, *as soon as* you find yourself in a transition situation, begin to work or read in the way that you had planned. If you don't get started right away, the chances are the transition will quickly pass by you and your opportunity to use it productively will be lost.

What's the potential for this way of using transition time? Remember, we're assuming that you have eighteen hours of transition time every week. If you use only ten of them for working or reading, you'll most likely be able to finish *all* of your newspaper or magazine reading for the week; or you'll complete ten hours of work time that you'd otherwise have to do elsewhere. You can see the implications of this approach for your efforts to achieve the four-hour day: if you can reduce a forty-hour work week to thirty hours through an aggressive use of ten hours of transition time, you'll be faced with only thirty hours of work to do elsewhere. This means that during your normal working periods, you'll only have to do the equivalent of six hours of work per day (six hours times five days equals thirty hours).

2. PLANNING

One of the most important time-savers is prior planning of time use. Poor planning will cause you to get involved initially in an inefficient task rather than one that's easy to finish. Or you'll fall into the fallacy of tackling a job that shouldn't be a priority, such as one that has a later deadline than others. Good planning, on the other hand, will make it much more likely that you'll address your tasks in the proper order. You'll also be more likely to keep your daily schedule fine-tuned for maximum efficiency.

This planning function is especially appropriate when you have only a few minutes of transition time. It only requires a minute or two to pull out your daily planner and reevaluate how you've decided to put your day together. Most people who get into the habit of this sort of planning usually find that the schedule they have set up the previous week or day, or even earlier that morning, may need some adjustment. You may find you're running late and need to call ahead to notify your next appointment; or maybe you're ahead of schedule, a circumstance that can provide you with a gift of extra time in the middle of the day; or maybe a meeting has been canceled, or you've found that some work you thought was essential can be postponed for a while. Going through this process of rethinking your schedule several times a day can increase tremendously your ability to use your time well.

3. PREPARING

Another very effective use of short bursts of transition time is preparation, which could include last-minute preparations for some talk or other presentation, or undertaking a short, perhaps creative segment of a larger assignment. It only takes a couple of minutes to go over an outline or conceptualize a memo or report.

Another good use of transition time is to prepare yourself for effective listening. If you go into an important meeting with another person or a group of people and your mind begins to wander or you don't really feel a part of the discussion, the time spent in that meeting will be wasted. You'll either lose completely the benefits you could have gotten from it, or you'll have to retrace your steps and, in effect, set up another meeting to get the information you need. The time just before such a meeting can be quite valuable in affording you the opportunity to anticipate the direction of the discussion, prepare pertinent questions, or ponder for a few moments the needs and orientations of the people who will be attending. Effective listening is such an important prerequisite to achieving the four-hour day that we've devoted a substantial part of Chapter 12 to this subject.

4. ENERGIZING

Perhaps the most obvious good use of transition time is just to relax or unwind from the day's tensions. We all need a "breather" several times during the day to recharge our emotional batteries, maintain momentum, and enhance endurance. But what are the best ways to achieve a truly *energizing* bit of time?

First, an illustration of what doesn't work: a hard-driving advertising executive had decided to make pitches for accounts with three different companies. He was in such a hurry for the new business that he scheduled meetings with representatives of the three companies on the same day. Each of the presentations was to take about one hour, with one early in the morning, one late in the morning, and the third in the middle of the afternoon. The first two went quite well, though at the end of the second, the account executive was exhausted. He had been required to hurry from the first appointment to the second with an entourage of his creative staff in tow. Then he had to get "up" for the second appointment so that he could project a high level of enthusiasm for the ideas he was pitching. After the second appointment was finished, he went out for some lunch at a nearby restaurant, but he then made the mistake of trying to wedge a personal errand into his schedule before the third appointment. As a result, he took no time to relax or rest, and shortly after the third appointment began, he felt his energy level flagging significantly. As much as he wanted to display the same kind of enthusiasm he had in the first two meetings, he found he just didn't have the inner reserves to pull it off. Consequently, the last meeting fell flat, and the potential client was unimpressed.

Instead, he might have gone back to his office, which was not far away, closed the door, and taken a brief nap.

Yes, a nap! When you have important business hanging in the balance, no one in the office—including your boss—will worry that you're closing your eyes and catching a few winks to help you improve your performance.

What other ways can you energize yourself during these transition periods? Here are a few suggestions:

Employ relaxation techniques, such as meditation. One possibility is that you might achieve the "relaxation response," as identified by the Harvard Medical School's Dr. Herbert Benson. The relaxation response is a medically and scientifically researched phenomenon that results in such beneficial physiological changes as lower blood pressure, slower metabolism, and reduction of stress.

The response can be produced by following this procedure: (1) pick a focus word or short phrase that fits into your belief system (for example, "God is love," or "Peace," or "Shalom"); (2) set aside ten to twenty minutes (a typical amount of transition time); (3) close your eyes and assume a comfortable, sitting posture; (4) begin to breathe regularly, and repeat your focus word or phrase silently to yourself on the out-breath; (5) when extraneous thoughts or outside noises threaten to interrupt, as they always do, don't fight them; just gently turn away from them and return to your focus word. Using this method during your transition periods—even if you don't have a full ten minutes—can do wonders to restore your spirits and energy.

Do something that you know helps you relax or unwind. You may just enjoy reading a light magazine or even watching a little television. Some people find that feelings of being oppressed or overwhelmed by the day's activities can be dissipated by taking ten or fifteen minutes to flick from one TV channel to another.

Caution: We've mentioned that TV can be a terrible time-waster, and so using the tube as a relaxation or unwinding device can easily get out of hand. More than a few people sit down with the good intentions of spending only a few minutes to relax in front of the TV and don't get up until hours have passed! So before you use television as an antidote for fatigue or a lack of energy, you'd better know your own limits very well.

Learn to establish sanctuaries of solitude in your life. Too few of us spend adequate amounts of time alone, fortifying and building upon our belief systems. The ancient spiritual masters of all faiths have emphasized spending much time in solitary meditation and devotion in order to prepare oneself to deal successfully with the stresses and strains of everyday life. The same advice applies to us today.

5. CELEBRATING

This last use of transition time can be extremely helpful in lifting your mood and increasing your enthusiasm for the rest of the day's activities. Those who are upbeat, expectant, and enthusiastic about their work or volunteer activities tend to experience less stress and be more productive and efficient. Despite these benefits, however, *celebration*, as we're using the term, is a technique that is usually overlooked or neglected.

What do we mean by *celebration*? An important dimension of this concept involves completely changing your perspective on your current situation, so that you focus primarily on the positive, rather than primarily on the negative. We're not simply talking about a superficial form of "positive thinking" here, but about effecting an entire shift of your outlook on the events and people that surround you at a given moment. Many of us start off the day in a fairly positive frame of mind; but as the day wears on, the pressures, preoccupations, and worries multiply, so that by the early or mid-afternoon, we may begin to feel quite weighted down with the cares of the world.

One antidote to this process of succumbing to the creeping pressures of daily life is to locate some transition time in the middle of the day and devote it to focusing on what's good and beneficial. During this time of personal celebration it's essential to dwell *only* on positive, uplifting thoughts, not on any negatives. There will always be a temptation to let worries or depressing impressions creep in, but you should push them aside and return to the positive. Some use joke books to help them lift their spirits. Others seek out upbeat, supportive friends, who can offer encouragement or perhaps provoke a laugh or two. Whatever it is, if it works to help you celebrate your life, use it! Spending only a few minutes this way in the middle of a particularly trying day can go a long way toward completely changing a negative mind-set to a positive one. And with a more positive, upbeat, celebratory attitude will come more enthusiasm and a higher level of energy, which will enable you to maximize your use of the time at your disposal.

As you're learning to employ your transition time more effectively, you'll most likely encounter some of the obstacles to efficiency that we call "time barriers." These barriers—including procrastination, overwhelming paperwork, and a host of other factors—can rear their ugly heads at any point during your busy schedule. To achieve the four-hour day, it's necessary for you to learn how to eliminate or hurdle these time barriers through a set of responses that we're about to introduce.

Chapter Nine

Breaking Through the First Time Barrier: Personal Resistances

So far, you have reconsidered your understanding of time, and you now should have a firm, explicit grasp of what's important in your life and what's not. You also see the importance of organizing each day to help you achieve those goals that will further your basic life priorities. But to make your new understanding of time a practical part of your life, it's necessary to take things one step further— by incorporating some proven time-saving techniques into your daily schedule.

WHY IT'S TIME FOR SOME TIME-MANAGEMENT TIPS

You have made significant progress in the *macro-management* of your time, in that you've begun to restructure the big picture of your work and leisure life. Now you're ready to do some *micro-managing* by looking at the details of your schedule and identifying those specific points in the day where you can save extra minutes, or even hours. This process of streamlining the details of your day is *absolutely essential* if you expect to pare down wasted time and move toward the four-hour day.

A centerpiece of this streamlining of your schedule involves the elimination, or at least the reduction, of what we call the *time barriers* in your life. There are three sets of time barriers that we'll be discussing in this chapter and the two that follow:

- The barrier of *personal resistances*—including such factors as procrastination, poor concentration, and inefficient handling of deadlines.

- The barrier of *excessive paperwork*—including unmanageable mail and office chaos.

- The barrier of *other people*—including ineffective delegation, proliferation of meetings and committees, telephone intrusions, and other interruptions.

What exactly is the connection between eliminating some of these time barriers and your goal of achieving the four-hour day? Consider the experience of Allison, who holds a middle-management position in a large national corporation.

THE LINK BETWEEN ELIMINATING TIME BARRIERS AND THE FOUR-HOUR DAY

Allison, a thirty-five-year-old single woman, confronted four major time barriers in her daily life:

- Procrastination
- Phone interruptions
- Inefficiency in dealing with incoming mail
- An obsession with news reports in the papers, on radio, and on TV

Allison consistently got to work early, about 8:00 A.M., even though most of the other people in the office drifted in around 8:30. But she almost always failed to make good use of her early arrival. She spent about twenty minutes walking aimlessly around the office and then dawdling at the coffee machine. When she finally sat down at her desk with a cup of coffee, it was usually 8:20. For the next ten to fifteen minutes, she listened to a small portable radio she kept in her office and thumbed through the morning newspaper.

As the workday got under way, Allison took practically every call made to her, even though she had a secretary who was able to screen those calls. As a result, she spent, on average, about an hour and a half on business-related calls and about a half-hour on personal calls in the course of the day.

Perhaps the most obvious disaster in Allison's time management was her mail. When the day's mail was put on her desk, she immediately thumbed through it. Then, with the intention of going through it more carefully later, she put *all* of it in her in-basket (or, when the in-basket got too full, on a corner of her desk). As a result of this approach, the largest stack of papers on her desk was old mail. In going through her letters once in a preliminary fashion and several more times before finally disposing of them, she spent an average of about forty-five minutes a day on mail-related tasks.

When Allison had a free moment during the day, she invariably turned back to her newspaper or to one of the news magazines she always carried with her; or she turned on the portable radio she kept near at hand. After finishing one paper or magazine, she would buy another. This constant reading and listening took up an hour and a half, from the time she arrived in the office until she left for home. And as soon as she arrived home after her normal nine hours at work, the news-junkie behavior continued. She immediately turned on the TV and watched the latest news reports and cable news programs, a practice that spanned at least three to four hours a night.

Clearly, a number of habits were causing Allison to use her time in ways that were basically wasteful or unproductive. Here's how she managed to clear away these time barriers.

First, she identified that wasted half-hour at the beginning of the day and took decisive steps to rescue the lost time. One tactic involved a simple behavioral ploy to overcome her early-morning procrastination. She recognized that the most pleasant thing about those initial morning minutes was drinking her coffee. So when she arrived at the office, she immediately went to the coffee machine, poured a cup, and headed *directly* back to her desk. That was a fairly easy, painless change in her habits, because she found she could enjoy herself anywhere she placed her coffee cup. This way, she at least got herself out of the office kitchen and hallways and back into her working space.

Next, she allowed nearly twenty-five minutes before 8:30 A.M. for reading the newspaper—but with a personal commitment that this would be all the time she would devote to the paper that day. Also, she resolved not to carry around any magazines or read other periodicals until she arrived at home at night.

Some might argue that it would also have been better for her to wait until the evening to read her newspaper; or perhaps it would have been advisable to get up a little earlier and read it before work. Either of these suggestions would have given her the entire first half-hour of the day to get a head start on her work. But remember, we're dealing in realities here. It's one thing to say that, on paper, Allison would have been a lot more efficient if she devoted that first half-hour to work. But she knew her limitations. She realized that she had a deep need to know what was going on in the world and in the business community. In fact, she felt that she would have been at a disadvantage in her business dealings if she had failed to keep abreast of events. She also understood that if she tried to make too much of a change in her life—if she attempted to eliminate too large a chunk of her normal routine—she might give up the effort entirely. As it was, she managed to eliminate newspapers and magazines from her working day, except for a half-hour in the morning. This meant that during a typical workday, she was saving *one entire hour* that had previously gone to reading or listening to the radio.

Her next challenge was to become more efficient in dealing with her mail. She was drawn to the old, simple rule that it's best to touch every piece of mail only once. Following this approach, she had to make a final decision about each letter when she picked it up for the first time and dispose of the matter before she went on to the next piece of mail. "I actually began to play mind games with myself," she recalled. "I thought, 'I *can't* put this letter down without doing something about it. If I do, something terrible may happen to me!' " The approach worked. She got into the habit of throwing out junk mail immediately, dictating short answers to mail that required a response, and alerting her secretary or some other assistant to any necessary steps demanded by other letters. With this technique, she cut the average time she spent on her mail each day in half, down to about twenty minutes.

Finally, Allison found a way to deal more efficiently with her telephone interruptions. By analyzing the nature of her calls over a two-day period, she discovered that she spoke to a number of the callers two or three separate times before the matter at hand was resolved. Also, many of the calls didn't require an immediate response. So she directed her secretary to collect her calls and supply her with a list of the callers with messages three times a day (a voice mail system would have worked equally well to collect calls). She did, however, make certain exceptions to the system: Allison identified a limited number of individuals, including her boss and family members, as priority callers who were still to be put through to her immediately. The messages from everyone else were to be collected and dealt with as a group *three times a day*.

Also, her secretary was told to find out in every case what the callers wanted, take detailed messages, and try to resolve as many situations as possible before involving Allison. This way, Allison discovered that she didn't even have to return many of the calls. As a result of this revamping of her telephone communications, Allison found she was able to enjoy much longer periods of concentration on her work, increasing her efficiency considerably.

Allison decided not to try to tinker with her television watching and news reading at home—at least not until she was sure her other new work practices were firmly ingrained. But even without changing her home habits, she found that by overcoming the time barriers of procrastination, mail, telephone interruptions, and excessive news intake, she was now saving over three hours of working time each day. The savings included: about twenty minutes on her mail; an hour and a half on her telephone interruptions; twenty minutes on early-morning procrastination; and one hour on unnecessary news reports. The impact of these time savings on her daily schedule was dramatic. Now, instead of working nine hours a day, she finds she is working less than six hours. Of course, at this point she's still in her office for nine hours. But she is well on her way to achieving a four-hour day of actual work *by doing nothing more than eliminating four simple time barriers!*

There are, of course, many other time barriers than the ones that plagued Allison. As we've seen, she faced two personal time barriers (procrastination and addiction to news reports), one paperwork barrier (mail), and one people barrier (telephone interruptions). To understand the possible array of barriers in each of these categories, we'll now deal with each of the types of barriers in turn.

THE PERSONAL TIME BARRIERS

The time barrier of personal resistance includes a wide variety of internal factors, including emotional quirks and personality traits, which can result in chronic time-wasting. Here are some of the major *personal barriers* that we've encountered in counseling people about their time-management problems.

Personal Barrier #1: Procrastination

Almost everyone gives in at one time or another to the temptation to put off some task or responsibility that may seem hard or distasteful. You may delay sitting down to write a report because you know writing is hard work. Or you may put off making a certain phone call because you expect you're likely to get into a difficult discussion or argument with the person on the other end of the line. *How can you overcome this natural tendency to procrastinate?* There are a couple of ways to change your perspective and break through the barrier of procrastination.

First, you might try what we call *taking the offensive against procrastination*. Here's the way this approach works:

STEP ONE: Most people tackle hard tasks—including the first job confronting them in the morning—in a defensive or negative way. A number of thoughts may go through their minds, such as: "I'm not awake enough to be efficient this early, so I'll just ease along into the day until I hit my stride." Or: "I'm going to hate this task, so I'll just enjoy myself a little longer with my newspaper—the work will get done, one way or the other."

Instead of giving in to this negative, defensive mind-set, spend a few moments just after you arrive at work focusing on an affirmative, aggressive frame of mind. Use positive, on-the-offensive self-talk: "I'm going to *like* doing this report!" Or: "I'm looking forward to taking on this responsibility because I know I can finish it in record time!'' It's important to speak positively to yourself *even if you don't feel particularly positive*. Work yourself into an assertive, upbeat, confident state—and then *explode* into the task.

STEP TWO: If possible, take on your hardest or most distasteful task first. If you're facing a particularly difficult phone call, get it out of the way right at the beginning of the day. This way you won't have it hanging over you and distracting you as the day wears on. Or if you know you must get to work on an especially demanding or difficult assignment, such as a complex research report or a very sensitive letter, do that at the outset. Finishing such a tough piece of work will make the rest of the day seem easy in comparison. And even if you don't finish the project, making significant progress on it will provide you with a much lighter, more confident feeling.

STEP THREE: Set a substantial but realistic goal to accomplish by midday—and then move aggressively to finish that work as though your entire day were scheduled to be over by noon. Your attitude should be: ''I'm going to do a full day's work before lunch, and I'm not going to allow coffee breaks, telephone interruptions, or anything else to get in the way.'' If you can get rid of a significant portion of your work before lunch, you'll find that your afternoons will often seem more relaxed. Furthermore, you'll begin to develop the sense that you are actually capable of doing an entire day's work in only half a day—good practice for your eventual goal of working only four hours a day.

There are many other ways to deal with the problem of procrastination. These include a number of behavioral psychology techniques, such as putting your coffee cup on your office desk, as Allison did in the previous illustration. The idea is to transform the experience or perception of pain into pleasure. If you find that it's painful to sit down at your desk, then use coffee or some other "carrot" as an inducement to disregard the pain. If you put your mind to it, you should be able to come up with some rather creative solutions on your own that will be just right for your particular schedule.

Personal Barrier #2: An Inability to Concentrate

You may find that you can overcome procrastination and manage to take a seat at your desk or other workplace, only to have your mind begin to wander. Or the ideas just won't come. Or you can't seem to focus on the task at hand. This inability to concentrate is a common personal time barrier that can be overcome in a number of ways, including the following:

Learn to handle your "start-up time." When you begin a new project, or pick up an old one from the day before, there's always a "start-up" period that may range from a couple of minutes to a half-hour or more. During this transition phase, you work less efficiently than when you're well into a job. Here's a way to fight this time-robber:

1. Expect to move along more slowly during this initial phase of a project. Most people accelerate later. If your expectations are realistic, you'll be more relaxed and, in the long run, more efficient.

2. When you begin to develop momentum, don't stop!

Don't take lengthy breaks or place a telephone call to a friend or colleague. Take advantage of the momentum when you have it.

3. If possible, schedule fewer projects to do during the day so that you'll have fewer start-up periods. We're not talking about doing less work—just getting involved in fewer things.

4. Try not to work intensely for more than about four hours during the day. Most people run out of steam if they devote the entire day to such activity. They tend to find that four or five hours daily is the maximum amount of time they can work efficiently on projects that require a high level of concentration.

You can see the implications of this last point for the four-hour day. One of the reasons we've picked four hours as your daily work target is that this is about the longest period of time that you can work intensely on a regular, daily basis. Of course, it's quite possible to put in more concentrated time in a day if you're really under the gun to meet a particular deadline. But most people find that working intensely for four, or perhaps five hours in a day is all they can take, day in and day out.

Leap over your "worry hurdles." One of the biggest obstacles to concentration is a concern that pops into your mind but cannot be resolved immediately. These "worry hurdles" may distract you for hours, as you turn them over in your mind. For example, you may get a call from a client who says he's displeased with something about your service, but he can't go into detail about it until you meet the following day. There will be a tendency to keep thinking about that upcoming meeting, turning various potential discussions and other scenarios in your mind. How can you deal with this sort of distraction?

First, try to deal with the worry immediately. If you can resolve the situation right then, do so without delay.

Second, if there are still loose ends you have to wrap up related to the problem, list the things you need to do and possible courses of action on a memo pad. Committing your worries to paper tends to free your mind from turning them over and over.

Third, pick a date or time to deal further with the problem. If that means setting up an appointment with a colleague or client, do so.

Overcome poor concentration with a change of scene. Most people suffer occasionally from a wandering mind. Sometimes this lack of self-discipline may stem from becoming too familiar with your surroundings. You fall into certain unproductive habits in your office, and those habits get worse and worse—until you find you're wasting huge amounts of time every day in "spacing out." One cure is to change the scene where you work.

Try moving to an empty desk or office, to the conference room, or to some other location. This shifting of scenes will often break old patterns of time-wasting.

Caution: Be sure to choose a work-intensive place, where the temptation or opportunity to waste time will be limited. In other words, you probably wouldn't want to choose the office canteen or a TV lounge for serious writing or analysis.

Personal Barrier #3: Too Many Loose Ends

Many people waste time each day because a multitude of little distractions, unfinished tasks, and disruptions immobilize them. We often allow numerous small concerns to accumulate and paralyze us. Some of these include:

- Multiple work projects that have been started but not resolved.

- A tendency to become angry, confused, or otherwise distracted by misplaced items, such as lost keys, letters, or memos.

- Becoming absorbed on the spur of the moment by the personal problems of secretaries, assistants, or associates.

- Being confronted by unexpected and perhaps seemingly irrational demands by a boss.

A list of such potential distractions would be endless, but there are a few effective ways of dealing with all of them:

- Confront the distracting problems in your workday *one at a time*. Don't try to deal with them all at once.

- Formulate a basic plan ahead of time for resolving each challenge. For example, if you find you frequently are troubled by lost letters, keys, or other items, set down these two basic rules: Always try to have two copies of everything you tend to lose; and, if you do lose an item, look for it for *one minute* (check your watch) and then forget it!

- Chart alternate routes around a potential problem well in advance of the difficult situation. If you tend to misplace your telephone book or important contracts, you should not only have two copies of them; you should also have a secondary repository for the duplicates of the frequently lost items, such as a special shelf or drawer. Then, if you lose something, you can go directly to its twin, without having to worry for more than a few seconds about what you're going to do without the misplaced item.

Personal Barrier #4: Lack of Punctuality

At first, you might think that a lack of punctuality is more of a problem for other people—the ones you're sup-

posed to be meeting—than it is for you. But in fact, if
you're often late to meetings or appointments, you're putting yourself at an extreme disadvantage in managing your
time efficiently. Constant lateness in getting to meetings
or to work will cause you to feel rushed, frustrated, disor-
ganized, and out of control. You'll also *look* rushed or
confused to others. The result may be an inability to in-
spire confidence in others, as well as a hasty, inadequate
performance in discussions and too little time to get things
done. How can you overcome chronic tardiness? A number
of punctual people have offered these suggestions:

***Always allow time to make it to your next appoint-
ment on schedule.*** This may mean winding up the preceding commitment a little in advance. For example, if
you know it's going to take you five minutes to get to the
next appointment, arrange things so that you can walk
out of the preceding session with six or seven minutes
to spare.

Suggestion: A number of punctual people have found
that it helps to note in their schedule the anticipated
windup time for the prior meeting and the time it takes to
get to the next appointment. So your daily appointment
diary might read something like this:

3:00 P.M.	Appointment with Jones and Smith
3:45 P.M.	Begin to wind up meeting
3:50 P.M.	Leave Jones-Smith meeting
4:00 P.M.	Appointment with Johnson and Drake

***Notify those you are meeting with about the time
when you have to move on to your next appoint-
ment.*** This sort of prior notification lets the people in the
preceding meeting know that they and their concerns are
important to you but that you do have other commitments.

Most people are quick to honor your need to make your next appointment.

You might set your watch a few minutes ahead. Some people find that this technique works quite well for them, while others know that they tend to compensate for the extra few minutes. You'll have to monitor yourself to see if this approach suits your personality.

Find a way to intensify your responsibility to be punctual. One sales rep was frequently late to appointments—until she turned her difficulty into a form of meditation. She began to sit down at the start of each day and repeat several times to herself, "Punctuality is important. It's *extremely* important for me to be on time to my appointments today. I'll make a bad impression on others if I'm late; but I'll make a good impression if I'm punctual." After engaging in this positive self-talk, she underlined each of the starting times of her appointments in red. This ritual helped impress on her how much her business relationships and her personal reputation depended on her ability to be on time.

Personal Barrier #5: Deadline Oppression

If you're like most people, much of the anxiety or stress in your life probably arises from a failure to handle deadlines well. Most likely, you set some of your own deadlines, and others set the rest by placing various demands on you. The problem is that these deadlines are often established with little warning, and with minimal planning. Consequently, before you realize what has happened, you have committed yourself to more responsibilities than you can fulfill. Or at least, you can't fulfill them within the time limits you've accepted.

One devastating consequence for time management is that you tend to spend far too much time worrying about deadlines that have been missed—or *may* be missed. The stress accompanying this anxiety can cause fatigue and an inability to perform other tasks during the day efficiently. So if you find yourself experiencing significant deadline pressure, it's important to confront it directly and deal with it swiftly.

How "livelines" can relieve the pressure of deadlines. "Livelines" work this way: a deadline, by definition, presents a do-or-die cutoff point; a liveline, on the other hand, is a finishing point that you recognize from the outset to be flexible—or "alive," open to possible revision. The key thing in scheduling your time is to determine those jobs that must involve deadlines and those that can be scheduled with livelines, or flexible end points. The great fallacy that most of us fall into is that we assume that all our time goals must be deadlines. Then, when we fail to meet some of the deadlines, as we inevitably must, we become depressed and start thinking we're incompetent or lazy.

How to sugarcoat a delayed deadline. If you decide to turn a deadline into a liveline, you should always propose a *specific* alternate due date. With this approach, you'll let your boss, colleague, or client know that you mean business and you're not just stringing him along. But be sure that you're being realistic this time. Also, be sure to meet the new deadline. Otherwise, you'll acquire the reputation of a person who is unreliable when it comes to finishing work on schedule.

It's also essential to give the person who is involved in the about-to-be-postponed meeting or other work as much advance notice as possible. It won't do to walk into his or her office at the very last moment, an hour before the report is supposed to be turned in, and say, "I need a little more time." You're much more likely to receive a favorable response if you provide plenty of prior warning about your plans. In addition, when you ask for a delay, it frequently helps to explain the circumstances that are causing your problem—such as pressing deadlines from other projects or particular difficulties you've encountered in finishing the project in question.

Finally, try not to delay any given deadline more than once. If you have to postpone a project multiple times, the frustration level in the person on the receiving end will escalate. Similarly, it's wise not to hit the same person with postponement requests on several different projects. If you are given a delay on one, be sure you're on time with the next. That way, you'll guard against developing the reputation of being a person who can't seem to live up to deadline commitments.

Personal Barrier #6: The Big Job Blues

Sometimes a particular task may seem so huge that you may find yourself feeling tempted to give up before you even get started. You can't imagine how you'll ever finish the project or live up to the overwhelming responsibility. The tendency in this situation is to put the big job at the bottom of your priority list. In a way, this is a very special-ized form of procrastination, and the way to deal effec-tively with the barrier is to look upon yourself as a long-distance runner. An endurance racer, as fast as he may be, can't cover ten miles in thirty minutes. If he tries, he'll soon become winded and may not finish at all. So he has to *pace* himself over the ten-mile course to maximize his performance.

The same principle applies to you when you're confront-ing a huge or long-term task. Many of your big jobs may require several days, weeks, or even months of work. If you tackle the responsibility with unrealistic expectations about how fast you can finish it, you'll become discour-aged, frustrated, and anxious when you fail to achieve your goal. Your confidence may be so damaged that the next time you confront a long-term job, you may not be able to get started at all.

To deal with this pacing problem, take these steps:

STEP 1:   List the particularly big or time-consuming tasks you have to accomplish.

STEP 2:   Beside each task, jot down the date by which it must or should be finished.

STEP 3:   Next to the completion dates, indicate your pacing goal. These goals should reflect your estimate of how much you think you can *easily* accomplish each day and still finish the task on time. This estimate should be based on *reality*, not on how much you want to do, or how much you think you should do.

STEP 4:   The first day, proceed to do at least the minimum amount of work you've set for yourself on the task. If you can do more than the daily goal, fine. If you do less, that's okay too. Sometimes, even when we feel we're setting easy goals, we find that a job takes more time and effort than we had imagined in the abstract. In such a case, it will be necessary to revamp the work schedule, and if necessary, see about adjusting the final deadline. Remember, the sooner you can notify your client or boss about problems you're encountering in meeting a projected deadline, the easier it will be to secure agreement on changing the due date.

STEP 5:   Keep slogging away at the project day after day, doing at least the minimum amount of daily work you've set for yourself. If you stay on this path, you'll find that before long—probably before your projected due date—the task will be completed.

By learning to hurdle each of these personal time barriers, you'll most likely find you're saving hours every week. Right now, don't worry about exactly what you're going to do with those hours. Just relax and enjoy yourself as your day becomes less cluttered and pressured.

The reduced stress and increased efficiency are a harbinger of what you'll eventually experience in an even more satisfying way when you attain your goal of the four-hour day. In fact, by overcoming these personal time barriers, you've just taken some significant strides toward making the four-hour workday an achievable part of your life.

Now let's move on to the second major time barrier that robs you of valuable hours every week—the barrier of paperwork.

Chapter Ten

Breaking Through the Second Time Barrier: Paperwork

You may be losing hours from your schedule each week because you're encountering an ocean of paper-related roadblocks to efficiency. These include:

- Out-of-control mail
- Inefficient telephone listings
- Fundamental problems with the way you've organized your office space
- A failure to make good use of lists
- "Time toys," such as the fax and cellular phones, which are often misused

Although each of these items, taken separately, may seem insignificant in the life of a busy manager, executive, or professional, they all have the power to undercut your daily efficiency and to put the four-hour day out of reach. Here are some suggestions for hurdling these paperwork barriers.

Paperwork Barrier #1: Mountains of Mail

It's usually a pleasant relief to receive mail at work. Unless you're dealing with an irate client or a lawsuit, you probably find thumbing through your mail—even the junk mail—to be a pleasant distraction from the demands of regular work. And there's a real bonus (and potential time-waster) when a magazine or a personal letter comes in with the business correspondence. Too often, though, the mail break may take a half-hour or longer, when it should usually require no more than about ten to twenty minutes. Here's a method to overcome the time-wasting temptations that may accompany your morning mail:

First, when you're ready to start dealing with the mail, get out of your chair and *stand up next to a trash basket.* If you must sit, don't retreat to an easy chair. Deal with your mail at your desk. The more you relax doing this task, the longer you're likely to take. Another important preliminary preparation is to place a letter opener near at hand to increase your speed and avoid messy letter edges for filing.

Second, as you begin to go through the mail, divide it into four action piles:

- Trash basket pile (Actually, this pile should go *immediately* into the trash basket and not become a separate pile on the desk. The faster you dispose of your mail, the more time you'll save.)
- Act-now pile
- Act-later pile
- Pile for magazines, newsletters, and other reading matter

Third, be decisive and ruthless in sorting your mail. Put as much as possible into the trash and the "act-now" pile. A proven technique at this stage of sorting is to touch each piece of mail only once. If you know you won't get a second chance, you're more likely to make quick decisions. If you don't act quickly on most of your mail, you'll have to waste time going through it a second time several hours or even days later.

Fourth, immediately after you sort out the magazine and reading-matter pile, put it out of reach. Don't read them now! If possible, choose a location such as your briefcase, where you'll be able to locate that material later. Remember, magazines and other reading matter may be attended to during transition times, such as when you're waiting for a meeting to begin, or during your commute.

Fifth, respond to the "act-now" pile *now*. If you postpone action, even for a few hours, you may forget precisely how you were going to respond to a specific letter. It's a waste of time—and annoying—to try to figure out for a second time how you're going to deal with a piece of correspondence.

Sixth, arrange to have the act-later letters filed, and if it's appropriate, enter a time and date on your daily calendar to indicate when you'll deal with them. It also helps to attach a note to each letter with a word or two to remind yourself or your secretary how the correspondence should be handled.

The best executive mail-handlers go through their newly arrived correspondence at top speed, as though they were dealing cards in blackjack. When sorting through your mail, keep a watch near at hand and note the time you begin and the time you end. It may even be useful to try to set speed records for getting through your mail. Otherwise, you could easily find yourself wasting a huge portion of your mornings on this task.

Paperwork Barrier #2: Untidy Telephone Numbers and Address Listings

It's possible for you or your assistant to waste valuable minutes every day if you lack an efficient method of retrieving phone numbers and addresses. The obvious devices are a Rolodex and a portable telephone book. But are yours up to date? Here are four simple suggestions that may help you improve your current system:

1. Your Rolodex should be straightened out and updated at least once a month—or more often if you accumulate new telephone numbers frequently. Slip-

ping odd-shaped pieces of paper into a Rolodex will work for a few days, or even a few weeks. But when this device is long neglected, it begins to look as though it's "growing" extraneous slips of paper and should be reorganized as soon as possible. Otherwise, you'll find yourself losing or misplacing valuable telephone numbers and addresses.

2. Keep and update a portable telephone and address book that you can carry with you to appointments. As much as possible, this book should duplicate the information in your office Rolodex. This way, if you lose the telephone book, you can always reconstruct it from the Rolodex.

3. A time-saving tip for both Rolodexes and portable phone-address books: personal telephone and address books frequently get messy and scratched up as people change addresses and phone numbers. To reduce the confusion and keep address books and Rolodexes clear and more serviceable, some executives have found it's helpful to write only the names of the people in pen. All the address and phone information is inserted in pencil. In this way, you can keep the names permanently in your directories, and when somebody moves, you can simply erase the old address and phone number and insert the new one— once again, in pencil.

4. If you use a portable electronic planner or office computer to keep your addresses, be sure you keep a duplicate disk or other file with the same information. When the batteries fail on many portable systems, the address material may be damaged or lost. A similar danger exists, of course, when a computer crashes.

Paperwork Barrier #3: An Unfriendly Office

An office may be "unfriendly," or unsuitable for your style of work, for two reasons: it may be too cluttered, *or* it may be too neat. A couple of old adages reflect this paradox. One says, "A cluttered desk means a cluttered mind." But another suggests the opposite: "An empty desk means an empty mind." Interestingly enough, *both* of these can be correct, depending on the kind of person you are and the approach to work that you prefer.

The cluttered vs. the neat office. There's an ongoing dispute among those who consider themselves time-management experts—and also among those who write time-management books—about how neat you need to be to operate at maximum efficiency. Some say it's impossible to be completely efficient unless your desk is clear and every item in your office is quite orderly and neat. Others argue, however, that it's best to accept some degree of clutter to keep necessary information and items near at hand, for immediate access. These views reflect two types of individuals, which we've identified as the "micro-neat" and the "macro-neat" personalities.

The micro-neat worker. These people always put everything away and always keep a clean desk in the office and a clean bureau at home. They are highly attentive to the details of personal order and naturally tend to file loose papers in their precisely proper place. Although they are often quite efficient in their work, they sometimes become so concerned about attending to minor details that they may devote too little time to the most important tasks. As a result, these people may fail to progress at full speed toward realizing the main priorities in their work and life.

The macro-neat worker. These people may look untidy, because they have mounds of files and papers on their desk. Also, books and other materials may be lying here and there on the floor. But they usually know exactly where everything is because they group their materials in broad (macro) categories as they arrange them on their desk, chairs, or shelves. The problem with the macro-neat worker arises when he or she ends up with too many "macro" piles and they start overlapping and getting mixed up with one another. It's at this point that productivity and efficiency may become impaired.

The challenge for you is to determine which category you fall into, and then approach your office organization accordingly. Above all, don't feel guilty if you're not as neat as one or more of your colleagues. As long as you're operating efficiently, feel free to use the floor, the desk, or any other part of your work space any way you choose.

Of course, you don't want to confuse the macro-neat personality with the totally sloppy worker who not only appears to be but really *is* unorganized. If you just throw materials here and there without giving any thought to keeping them in some sort of order for later use, you will surely encounter serious time-management problems.

How Can You Tell If Your Office Is Becoming Too Sloppy?

Here's a checklist of danger signals, with some suggestions, for the macro-neat worker who may be on the verge of becoming macro-messy.

DANGER SIGNAL #1:   Your important papers and notes always seem to get wrinkled or creased.

SOLUTIONS: Keep more of this important information on a computer. For things you have to keep on paper, get a Pendaflex-style lateral filing system, which allows you to suspend all your files in the filing cabinet. This way they won't "float" down under one another and become wrinkled.

DANGER SIGNAL #2:   You misplace telephone messages, bills, or other pieces of paper at least once a week.

SOLUTIONS: Have your secretary or assistant use electronic mail for telephone messages, so that the message appears on the computer disk. Or buy telephone note pads that allow you to make a copy of each message. Then you can stuff the message into your pocket for later reference with the confidence that you're protected if you lose it.

Loss of other important papers probably indicates that the flow of papers from your secretary to you and back to your secretary is inefficient, *or* that your filing system is ineffective. Do a brief systems analysis of your office to see if there's a bottleneck—anyone's desk where papers lie around for more than an hour. All correspondence, bills, and other documents should be put immediately into a safe file. If the main problem is with your files, you may be violating the basic principle of filing: that all items should be *immediately retrievable*.

DANGER SIGNAL #3: You always seem to be missing pens, pencils, paper clips, paper, or some other necessary item.

SOLUTIONS: Every item in your office should have its own "home." If you haven't designated a special place for your supplies, do so today and inform your secretary of the spot. Many minutes can be saved by this simple step.

DANGER SIGNAL #4: You sometimes spend more than two minutes trying to find a book in your library.

SOLUTIONS:

Poorly organized libraries are one of the worst problems faced by workers or executives who have to do frequent research or checking of references. You can completely lose a train of thought in preparing a speech or report if you spend ten or fifteen minutes looking for some important book. If you have a large library in your office, the books should be grouped into major sections and then alphabetized by author within each section. Clippings, statistics, and other facts that you frequently use should be given an easily accessible home in your files (or on your computer).

DANGER SIGNAL #5:

Important projects seem to remain unfinished or untouched at the end of many working days.

SOLUTIONS:

If you frequently seem to fail to do all you feel you should do on important jobs, you might establish a set of priority folders in your office for use each working day. You or your secretary can then put the most important materials and reminders in the "first priority" folder, the less pressing things in the "second priority" folder, and so on. In this way, you'll have your day clearly structured and you won't feel so frustrated if you fail to get through the lower-priority folders.

DANGER SIGNAL #6:

There is a pile of papers more than one inch high in your in-box at the end of many working days.

SOLUTIONS: One radical solution is not to have an in-box at all. Remember the methods we suggested for handling your mail: deal with things *immediately* as they come in. Some may be placed in an out-box for disposal by secretaries or other assistants. If you do use an in-box, try to clean it out each day. Otherwise, there is a strong likelihood that things will accumulate and sit there for days or weeks. (We know one entrepreneur who found a one-year-old check for nearly $1,000 at the bottom of his in-basket!)

DANGER SIGNAL #7:   Papers are piling up on your desk—on the upper-right-hand section for right-handers, or on the upper-left-hand section for left-handers.

SOLUTIONS: In general, if these piles begin to grow day by day, you can take that as an indication that you need to set aside a few minutes (or hours, if necessary) to dispose of the accumulation. The sooner you act, the better, because stacks of papers that you fail to deal with now will be much larger and probably take more time to handle later.

        Of course, if you're a macro-neat person, you may prefer to work with a slightly cluttered desk. If you're involved in an ongoing project, it will probably be inefficient to clean up your desk or other working spaces at the end of every day and then lay out the same materials the next morning. You could lose ten or fifteen minutes a day going through this unnecessary pick-up, put-down procedure. But there often comes a point at which efficient stacking and spreading-out degenerates into clutter and confusion. When you find yourself allowing items to pile up on your desk and you realize that you're not working daily on those items, you're on the road to organizational trouble in your office.

Paperwork Barrier #4: A Lack of Good Lists

Paperwork and other responsibilities in the office can get out of control if you fail to list the items you have to do, and the time and place where you must do them. There are three devices that can help you stay on track with your daily schedule:

1. A *desk diary*, which contains times and places for all your appointments and other responsibilities. The style that displays one full week when you open the book flat is one of the most popular and useful.

2. A *pocket diary*, which is just a small version of the larger desk diary. With the pocket diary, you'll always have access to your schedule, even when you're away from the office. If you use it in conjunction with a desk diary, your secretary will have access to your schedule while you're away, and you'll always have a back-up in case you lose the pocket diary.

3. A *"to-do" list*, which is simply a slip of paper listing the main work projects you expect to finish or make progress on during the day. The to-do slip should be prepared at the beginning of each day, and the items on it should be listed in order of their priority. Usually, only work goals are included on

this list; appointments and meetings go into the pocket diary. Be sure to save each day's list for at least one day before you throw it out, because the previous day's list can be helpful in preparing the list for the current day. You'll often find that there is a carry-over of items from one day to the next, especially if you're involved in one or more long-term projects.

Of course, it's possible to write this to-do list in your pocket diary. But many people feel that adding such a list to the same space that contains information on daily appointments can result in excessive messiness and confusion. For this reason, we recommend that you keep your to-do list separate from the entries on your pocket diary.

Paperwork Barrier #5: Untamed Time Toys

Finally, be sure to evaluate your use of "time toys," such as the fax, cellular phones, and beepers, which are supposed to save time but may in fact do the opposite. Even the computer may fall into this category. You may find that it's easier and faster to use handwriting for some purposes than to have to input the information into a computer and then retrieve it every time you want it. Or you may discover that you're faxing memos when you could just as easily (and more cheaply) use the mails or the telephone. Or you may feel that the portable phone you carry around with you is becoming intrusive and robbing you of important periods of isolation and silence. Just because a technological innovation makes things move faster doesn't necessarily mean the device is making things better or more efficient for you. Used properly, the fax, the cellular phone, and the computer can be great time-savers. But be sure that you control them; don't let them take control over you!

Now, let's move on to the final time barrier—the people in your life who may be causing you to waste huge chunks of your workday.

Chapter Eleven

Breaking Through the Third Time Barrier: Other People

The third and last time barrier that may interfere with your efficiency and block your progress toward the four-hour workday is a barrier that involves other people.

There are at least five major mini-barriers that may make up this particular roadblock to successful time management:

- Misuse of the telephone
- Too many meetings
- A proliferation of committee assignments
- The inability to say no
- A failure to delegate properly

Here are some thoughts about how these problems may arise—and what you can do about them.

People Barrier #1: Misuse of the Telephone

One of the greatest thieves of your time may very well be the telephone—or, more specifically, the people you talk to during the day on the phone.

One attorney allowed his secretary to put through practically every call that came in to him during the day unless he was in a meeting or on another call. As a result, he found himself not only fielding questions from clients and potential clients, but also dealing personally with solicitations from stockbrokers, insurance agents, and all manner of salespeople. These telephone interruptions were costing him an average of an hour and fifteen minutes per day. In addition, he lost even more time having to "shift mental gears," as he went from working on one of his cases to a phone call and back again to the case.

After identifying this time-waster, the lawyer cut back drastically on the telephone calls he took directly during the day. He had his secretary collect many of his calls, except those that involved pressing matters from important clients. As a result of this restructuring of his telephone practices, the attorney managed to save more than an hour a day in phone misuse.

People Barrier #2: Too Many Meetings

It's been estimated that top-level executives typically spend up to 70 percent of their working time each day in meetings. Although there's nothing necessarily wrong with this allocation of time, these two qualifications should be kept in mind: (1) the meetings should make a direct contribution to the health of the organization; and (2) they should be the most effective way of dealing with the issues under consideration.

When you're evaluating your situation, you should keep in mind the advantages and disadvantages of meetings in helping you do your work efficiently. The chances are good that meetings will work *against* your effectiveness if you're a hands-on type of worker or manager, the type who tends to become directly involved in tasks rather than delegating the work to others. So if you are a lawyer, technical expert, creative type in an ad agency, or other professional, you may find that you produce more when you're alone or working with a small, task-oriented team. If this sounds like your situation, you should do all you can to avoid unnecessary meetings.

On the other hand, if you're a high-level manager or executive, you may need to spend more time in meetings so that you can monitor the work of those under you and guide them as they deal with their responsibilities. But even if this description fits, you shouldn't assume automatically that formal, regularly scheduled meetings are the best route to take. Regular meetings may be helpful, but they may also degenerate into a waste of time. It's essential for the person calling the meeting to keep reevaluating their helpfulness. If it becomes evident that a certain type of meeting isn't accomplishing much, the best solution is usually to discontinue it.

Research by time-management experts Stephanie Winston, Henry Mintzberg, and others has revealed that the most successful executives spend nearly 80 percent of their time talking with other people—but about half of these encounters average less than ten minutes each, and only 10 percent go on longer than an hour. A number of executives report that informal discussions, including brief chats with "drop-ins"—people just pop into the boss's office for some advice—seem to accomplish a great deal—and may even be more valuable than regularly scheduled meetings. (This argument has been made forcefully by Alan Deutschman in "The CEO's Secret of Managing Time," *Fortune*, June 1, 1992.)

Warning: Drop-ins can be a two-edged sword. If you become too accessible to other people in the office, you'll find yourself in the same trouble as those who take too many phone calls. Most workers probably need to maintain a closed-door policy for several hours during the day so that they can finish their assignments as quickly as possible. If you're a high-ranking executive and want to try an open-door policy, just be sure that you're alert to the need to *close* your door when intense concentration is required.

People Barrier #3: Committee-itis

Almost every competent, active, socially concerned person has encountered the problem of getting involved in too many committees, both at work and during non-work hours. These "little" commitments can accumulate to the point where they seem to leave little time for anything else.

Many times, you don't have a choice about whether or not you serve on committees at work, especially if your boss has directed or "asked" you to serve. Unfortunately, committee assignments involve not only meetings—a problem already discussed under People Barrier #2—but also paperwork and reports. Sometimes, it's an honor to serve on a company committee, especially those executive committees that make policy or wield significant clout in the organization. But if you feel your committee assignment is largely unnecessary or time-wasting, here are some suggestions for minimizing your involvement:

- Don't volunteer for assignments that require written reports, such as minutes.

- If you have to produce written material, keep it as short and to the point as possible. Everyone will appreciate your brevity, and you'll save yourself and your secretary a lot of time.

- Don't volunteer for subcommittee assignments. If you do have to serve on a subcommittee, try to avoid becoming chairman, a role that usually takes more time than just being a member.

- If you feel your committee roles are cutting into your other work time too much, be assertive in discussing the problem with your supervisor. When you go in to see him, be prepared to provide details that show exactly how much time you're spending on your committees. Also, be ready to suggest responsibilities that you might cut back on or eliminate entirely.

How do you know if you've caught the committee-itis disease on the job? Calculate the time you spend in committee meetings and committee work during your office hours. You should include committees that involve extra-curricular activities in the office, such as organizing holiday parties. If you find that you average more than an hour a day on this work-related committee activity, that's probably too much for you to operate at maximum efficiency. (An exception to this rule would be the situation where much or most of your job description involves performing committee assignments.)

Non-work committees. You have more control over committee involvements that are completely voluntary, such as those in charitable or volunteer organizations. To evaluate your situation and see where you might reduce your involvement, follow these steps:

1. List all the non-work committee meetings that you attend during one month.

2. Beside each of these commitments, indicate the number of evenings (and also full days) that you devote to each commitment.

3. Add up the total number of evenings and full days devoted to these meetings, and figure out the percentage of your waking hours during the month that you are devoting to them. (If you attend some meetings less frequently than once a month, add up the total amount of time you spend at such meetings during the course of a year. Then divide by twelve to get the average monthly commitment.)

This analysis will provide you with a fairly accurate picture of whether or not you're a victim of "creeping committee-itis" during your non-work hours. As a rule of thumb, if you're spending more than five nights or two complete days a month on volunteer committee work, you've moved into the committee-itis danger zone.

People Barrier #4: A Failure to Say No

If you feel you're being overloaded with work, you may have to draw a line at additional assignments by saying, in effect, "I'm sorry, but I just don't have time available to handle that." Of course, the *way* you convey this message will depend on who is trying to get you to take on more responsibilities. If you're being asked by someone to take on a voluntary activity, such as a duty at your church or synagogue, and you feel you already have too much to do, you should just say no in a nice way.

It's not easy for certain people to turn others down, especially when they are approached to help out with a worthy cause. If you fall into this category, you'll have to consider the alternatives: If you do take on too much, what will happen to your family life? What compromises will you have to make with other responsibilities? How will you handle the extra pressure? By considering seriously what will happen if you take on the extra activity, you'll develop a more realistic perspective on the consequences, and it will be much easier to say, "Sorry, you'd better try someone else."

If you're confronted with excess duties at work, the situation becomes more complicated. You certainly have the power to control your time if a peer at work or a client asks you to do something. You'll have to consider a number of issues, such as whether you'll alienate a coworker whom you may want to ask for help yourself at a later time. You'll also have to weigh the loss of business from a client if you turn her down. But still, you have the power to organize your work load, and after analyzing your situation, you should exercise that power.

The most difficult situation arises when your *boss* asks, or tells, you to take on a project that seems too burdensome. In such circumstances, it's often not easy to say no because of a fear that a negative response may convey laziness or a lack of serious commitment to the job. On the other hand, being assertive in this sort of situation may work well if you follow a procedure that assures your boss of your commitment but at the same time makes him aware of the total array of pressures you're facing. Here's one possible approach:

- When your boss approaches you about taking on a new assignment, respond positively, but ask for some time to study the proposal and to see how it fits into your other commitments.

- If you determine that you don't have sufficient time to take on the extra load, draft a memo to your boss indicating in some detail the other responsibilities you have and the amount of time that they take.

- Conclude the memo with a recommendation about how to deal with the new responsibility. If you feel you shouldn't get involved in it at all, say so. If you've sensed that this new project is of overriding importance to your boss, suggest that you might be able to handle it if you can drop or cut back on some of your other responsibilities. Or if you feel you could do part of the new project, propose a limited commitment of some sort.

Obviously, you don't have total control over your time when you're dealing with assignments from your supervisor or superior. But you *do* have the power to make a cogent, rational case about how taking on too many duties can undercut your effectiveness in the organization. A well-reasoned, properly presented memo—one that says no or "only under certain circumstances" in a deferential, intelligent way—will often be all that's required to prevent your becoming overloaded at the office.

People Barrier #5: Failure to Delegate

Much has been written in various management and business books about the virtues and skills of delegation, and we certainly don't propose to treat the subject comprehensively in the next few paragraphs. But because the skill of delegating effectively is absolutely essential to an optimal use of time, we want to suggest the following principles that underlie the approach of many adept delegators.

PRINCIPLE ONE: Notify the person to whom you plan to delegate a task well in advance of the time when the task is scheduled to begin. Our experience, as well as the research of behavioral psychologists, indicates that people who are informed in advance, and who also commit themselves in advance, are more likely to complete the task successfully. Conversely, if you tell a person without any prior warning that he or she will have to take on a significant new job, it's likely that you'll receive a negative response.

PRINCIPLE TWO: Effective delegation requires that the nature of the task to be delegated be clearly defined and that the person respond in definite terms. He might say, "Sure, I understand what you want and I'll have it ready by the due date." Or if he has a time problem, he may negotiate for less work or a more distant due date. In any case, be sure that the two of you have the same, definite understanding about what work is to be done and when it is due.

PRINCIPLE THREE: Positive reinforcement helps ensure the success of the delegation. You might take your staff member out to lunch at different times when she finishes successive phases of the work. Or you

might present her with a small gift at
the end of the task. Perhaps the most
effective (and least expensive) kind of
positive reinforcement is to compliment
her work at different stages and tell her
how much you appreciate her.

With these basic principles in mind,
you might want to use the following
simple checklist, which has worked for
many managers who delegate important
tasks to a secretary:

Set up priorities for his work. Unless you tell your
secretary clearly what's important and what's not, he's
likely to concentrate on peripheral things and fail to perform key tasks.

Don't do your secretary's work. It's important to keep
your priorities separate from his. A key rule in effective
delegation is to give your subordinates complete responsibility for the jobs you assign them rather than constantly
looking over their shoulders.

Prepare your secretary's day before he arrives. Many
managers waste an hour or more of secretarial help each
day simply because they wait until he arrives before they
begin thinking about what he should do. Try to stay a
couple of days ahead of your secretary and establish set
routines. This way, if you're not in the office or haven't
had time to prepare for him on a given day, he'll still
have work to do.

Use a dictating machine for correspondence. You'll
save hours on your letters if you learn to dictate short
letters into either a regular dictating machine or a tape
recorder. Drafting your own correspondence will take at
least two to three times as long as using a dictating device.
Also, it's usually more efficient to use a recorder for dicta-

tion than to call your secretary in to take dictation. You
can do your dictating into a recorder during your transition
time. Also, you'll conserve your secretary's time by
allowing him to focus just on typing the letters, rather than
on taking dictation *and* typing.

Have your secretary screen your calls. This is one of
the most common and effective uses of delegation with
a secretary.

***Confront your secretary's time-wasting immediate-
ly.*** If he is chronically late to work, hangs on the telephone for long periods with personal calls, or otherwise
wastes time, call him into your office for a frank talk. It's
best to get these feelings of dissatisfaction out into the
open as soon as possible so that they won't fester and
undercut your working relationship.

***Allow your secretary to work as much as possible
in the areas of his natural interests.*** For example, if
he likes bookkeeping and you need a bookkeeper, make
that a part of his responsibilities.

These people-oriented obstacles are the last of the three
major time barriers that you'll face during the course of a
typical day. But there's more to good time management
than just getting rid of roadblocks. On the more positive
side, you can actually accelerate your level of efficiency
by honing what we've called the "three basic speed
skills"—speed reading, fast writing, and effective
listening.

Chapter Twelve

The Three Basic Speed Skills

After you've eliminated or minimized the time barriers in your life, you may have found that you've been able to reduce your working time considerably, say from eight or nine hours a day to six. Somehow, though, you can't seem to break through that six-hour barrier. You know that the four-hour day will remain out of reach unless you find a way to increase your efficiency.

So what's the next step you should take to reduce your working hours even more? The answer is to focus on *accelerating your speed* in accomplishing important tasks. Specifically, you should concentrate on developing three fundamental speed skills:

- speed reading
- fast writing
- effective listening

To get some idea about what these skills can do for you, consider the challenge that confronted Paul, a researcher working for a local municipality.

HOW PAUL REVVED UP THE PACE
OF HIS WORK

Paul, an experienced official in city government, was an expert in environmental problems and had pursued graduate studies in ecology and related scientific fields. He preferred getting directly involved in research, and so he was often assigned to head study projects on the environment in his locality. Often when he was in the midst of these assignments, he felt that the work was taking too much time. He found that he was regularly putting in eleven- or twelve-hour days, and this heavy schedule left him little time for outside interests.

In analyzing his time use one day, he discovered that he devoted about four hours to reading and studying various reports, articles, books, and other written sources. Then he turned to writing up some of the information he had been gathering, and he found that that process required about three hours. Finally, he conducted interviews with a couple of experts on the topics he was researching, and those discussions required another two hours. When Paul added the above work time to the one hour of administrative time he had to put in, he saw why he was spending about ten hours in the office every day. So what could he do about it?

He had been rather effective in eliminating many of the time barriers that we discussed in the previous three chapters. So he suspected that any inefficiency might lie in one or more of the major speed areas we've just identified: reading, writing, and listening. Paul studied his style of reading, writing, and interviewing to see if there was anything he could do to cut down on the time he was spending in these areas without hurting the quality. Here's what he discovered, and what a time expert advised him to do:

- In his reading, he was plowing through every piece of material from beginning to end.

Speed recommendation: Scan each piece of material first, and then read it more closely. This approach provides a better overall grasp on the material before the in-depth reading begins. In almost every case, the end result is faster digestion of the material.

- In his writing, he usually plunged right into his draft, with little or no attempt to outline or organize before he started.

Speed recommendation: *Always* put your notes in the order that you expect them to appear in your write-up, and *always* draft an outline of the major points you expect to make before you ever sit down to write.

- During the interviews he conducted, he spent about one fourth to one half of his time regaling the interviewees with his own views.

Speed recommendation: When you're trying to get information from others, focus on listening rather than talking. You already know what you believe and what information you possess. Devote most of the time to allowing the other person to express his views and convey his materials. You can always merge your opinions into his views later when you begin to write.

By making these simple adjustments, Paul cut his work time by these amounts: his daily reading time dropped, on average, from four hours to two hours; his writing time decreased from three to less than two hours; and his listening time went down from two hours to one hour. The total time he saved through these speed changes was *more than four hours a day*. This reduction meant that his average work time decreased almost immediately from ten hours a day to less than six. Furthermore, he continued to pare down his work time by increasing his speed in reading, writing, and listening, and soon was well on his way to achieving the four-hour day.

Paul's accomplishment in revving up the pace of his workday is an improvement available to anyone who observes a few simple principles. As you move through the following pages, we also want to encourage you to pursue developing these skills on your own. Now, let's consider in more depth the first speed skill: high-velocity reading.

The First Speed Skill: High-Velocity Reading

Most people read far too slowly—at an average of 250 words per minute, according to surveys made by such programs as the Evelyn Wood speed reading system. But with some simple techniques, it's possible to double or triple your reading speed almost immediately. And by taking a speed reading course—and working hard at it—you can go much faster than that. Here are some basic techniques that can hike your reading speed significantly the very next time you pick up a book or article:

1. Always plan to go over reading material at least twice and preferably three or four times.

2. Use your hand or finger to pace yourself as you read. This way, you will be less likely to regress, or read back over material you've already looked at.

3. The first time through, read the material *fast*, in a scan mode. Whether it's a book or a short article, spend no more than about five seconds on each page. This way, you'll go through a twelve-page article in one minute, or a 360-page book in a half-hour. Don't worry about comprehending everything in this initial run-through. You'll most likely comprehend no more than a third to a half of what you read. The main idea here is just to get a sense of the big picture of the source you're studying, the overall structure, and perhaps a few of the main points and conclusions. Focus on material that is in boldface or that is set off or highlighted in some way in the text. It's al-

ways helpful to look over the table of contents in this first phase of your reading.

4. Take a few moments to jot down some questions about the material that you want answered. These questions should be highly pragmatic. Remember, you're reading for a work purpose, not for pleasure. When you get the information you need, move on to your next task!

5. On the second and subsequent readings, slow down your pace, and begin to make notes or highlight material in the text. Read as slowly as necessary to enable you to comprehend what you need to know, but again, use your hand to pace your eye. With this method, you'll be more likely to maintain steady concentration throughout the reading. As you go through, try to find the answers to the questions you posed after the first reading.

6. As you become more comfortable with this technique, begin to play speed games with yourself. Look over the reading matter before you start and figure how fast you'll need to go to read more quickly than you've ever read before. Keep track of your progress with a watch.

Those who follow these simple reading strategies usually find that they can increase their reading speed by more than 100 percent with little practice. (For those who want to move up to 1,000 words per minute or beyond, a helpful resource is *Remember Everything You Read: The Evelyn Wood 7 Day Speed Reading and Learning Program*, by Stanley D. Frank.)

The Second Speed Skill: Fast Writing

Once you've read quickly through the printed material in your research, the next step is often putting the results down on paper, in the form of a report, memo, or letter.

You can increase the speed of your writing significantly through these techniques.

1. Organize all your notes in the order you expect them to appear in your written draft. It's usually best to keep separate thoughts, facts, and points on separate note cards. This way, you can shuffle them around and produce the order you prefer. When you have your research materials in order in front of you, you're ready to put them into outline form.

2. *Always* outline everything you write. We've found that a failure to outline increases the writing time by multiples as the length of your memo or report increases. The problem is that if you just sit down and begin to draft something, you'll inevitably place your facts in the wrong order or leave something important out. This tendency to make such mistakes increases as the length of your report increases.

   One of the most useful types of outlines for most writing projects is the simple three-part structure:

   I.   Introduction
   II. Body
   III. Conclusion

   Every piece of writing—whether report, memo, or letter—should have these three components. The best outlines, however, are more detailed. One approach is to list the main points you plan to make under *body* in any order in which they come to mind. Then, on a clean sheet of paper, reorder the points in the way you want to present them in your draft.

   Many good, fast writers go even further in their outlining. As part of their outline, they will write out the first two or three sentences that they plan to include in the *introduction*, and they may also write out a sentence or two for the *conclusion*. In addition, they include in the *body* subtopics and brief observations and insights they expect to make later in their draft. Remember, the more time you devote to your outline, the less time you'll spend writing your draft.

3. As you write, follow your outline closely and use it to form paragraphs and subsections. If you've put together a very detailed outline (even the most detailed will rarely run longer than two single-spaced typed pages), you'll find that your paragraphing and subsections fall naturally into place as you write. If you're writing a rather long item, say in excess of about 2,500 words, you'll probably find that the three or four main points you listed in the *body* will form natural subsections that can be set off in the text with subheadings. The subtopics under those main points may become paragraphs in your draft. It's usually wise to use many paragraphs in a written piece and also to signal major changes of thought or argument with subheadings. These devices enhance reading and make the basic organization stand out clearly.

4. Keep your sentences relatively short. A good rule of thumb is that a sentence that runs more than about three lines on a normal typed page is too long.

5. Learn to type or use a word processor if you don't already have these skills. Those who try to write, rewrite, and edit their reports and memos without a word processor are still living in the administrative dark ages. It will take a few weeks to become reasonably adept at a typing keyboard and to learn the basics of a word processing system. But you'll literally cut more than 50 percent off your writing time with these tools.

6. Always revise and proofread. If your memo or report is thrown back at you because you've failed to remedy illogical points, to remove redundancies, or to correct other errors, you'll spend extra time reworking the material, not to mention making a bad impression on your boss.

Now, having dealt with these two rather obvious speed concerns—of reading and writing—let's turn to a less well-known difficulty that can be speeded up: listening to other people.

The Third Speed Skill: Effective Listening

It was obvious to Paul, in the opening illustration in this chapter, that he could reduce his work time by becoming a more efficient listener in his interviewing. But listening well is a skill that can be helpful on a much broader stage than the formal interview. In your encounters with others during the day, you may be wasting many minutes or even hours by ineffective listening. Among other things, poor listening may cause you to make bad decisions that will have to be undone at a later date, to misunderstand what the other person is saying, or to miss completely some important information. There are four major areas where poor listening may be costing you time that you can't afford to lose out of your busy schedule. These include:

1. A failure to observe the ten basic rules of effective communication in any work or social situation.

2. A failure to discern techniques of persuasion that may prevent you from asking relevant time- and money-saving questions.

3. A failure to recognize roadblocks that are getting in the way of smooth communication.

4. An inability to perceive those weak points where communication breaks down.

Now, let's consider some ways that you can overcome these four problem areas and become a more effective and time-conserving communicator and listener.

THE TEN BASIC RULES OF EFFECTIVE COMMUNICATION

No matter whom you're talking to, be sure to observe every one of these fundamental rules. In most cases, following them will save you an amazing amount of time in the process of listening and communicating.

RULE #1:   Find areas of personal interest—and if necessary create them yourself. The bad listener will tune out dry subjects, even if they are important to achieving a high level of excellence in his work. The good listener will look for opportunities to become interested, even when the subject matter at first seems boring. He'll ask himself, "What's in this for me? How can I use what I'm hearing?"

RULE #2:   Judge the other person's content, not his delivery. The bad listener tunes out the other person if the delivery is poor. The good listener focuses on the content of the communication and skips over errors or flaws in delivery.

RULE #3:   Hold your fire until the other person is finished. The bad listener tends to enter into argument at any sign of disagreement with his own position. The good listener doesn't render judgment until he's sure he really understands what the other person is saying.

RULE #4:   Listen for ideas. The bad listener listens for facts. The good listener listens for central themes, or the ways that the facts are strung together.

RULE #5:   Be flexible in note-taking. The bad listener takes intensive notes and generally will employ only one type of note-taking, such as recording what's said in paragraph form. The good listener will take fewer notes and may use several different systems of note-taking, depending on the speaker.

For example, with a very logical, well-organized speaker, the good listener may use a structured, outline system of taking notes. But with an impressionistic or less well-organized speaker, the good listener may place main ideas in boxes on one or several sheets of paper. Then this note-taker may add to those boxes as the speaker returns periodically to a particular topic.

RULE #6: Work at listening. The bad listener shows no output of energy, and may appear to be faking attentiveness. The good listener will work hard to "crack" a subject he can't immediately connect with, and will exhibit active, genuinely attentive body language.

RULE #7: Resist distractions. The bad listener is distracted easily by outside events or noises. He's the type who will continue to answer his phone during a discussion, even though these interruptions seriously damage the flow of conversation. The good listener fights or avoids distractions, tolerates the other person's bad habits, and knows how to concentrate on the subject at hand.

RULE #8: Exercise your mind. The bad listener resists difficult, expository material, even when it's well presented. He only responds well to light, recreational material. The good listener views heavier, hard-to-understand material as a challenging exercise for the mind.

RULE #9: Keep your mind open. The bad listener reacts in a predictable way to emotional buzz words and concepts. The good listener doesn't become hung up on the words and concepts, but rather, attempts to interpret them in the context of the discussion.

RULE #10: Capitalize on the fact that thought moves much faster than speech. The bad listener tends to daydream when a speaker is moving at a slow pace. The good listener keeps his fast-moving mind on the subject under discussion. If the speaker is moving slowly, this listener will mentally challenge, anticipate, summarize, and weigh the evidence he's hearing. He'll listen between the lines by evaluating the other person's presentation and the tone of voice.

UNDERSTANDING THE TECHNIQUES OF PERSUASION

If you hope to save time as an effective listener, you'll have to become adept at cutting through the veneer of what the other person is saying, so that you can get to the heart of the issue. This skill is especially important if you're dealing with someone who is trying to convince you of something or sell you something. The effective listener will recognize persuasion techniques and be able to challenge them—at the proper time—with relevant questions. Getting the answers to these important questions is essential if you hope to make wise decisions and avoid having to undo mistaken courses of actions.

The six main persuasion techniques you should watch for are:

- *The bandwagon:* The would-be persuader will try to get you on board by saying, in effect, "Everybody's doing it!"
- *Card-stacking:* This approach involves the use of illustrations, facts, or opinions of supposed experts that

are carefully selected to make the best or worst possible case for a particular idea, product, or person.

- *Glittering generality:* A seller may associate his product with a virtue or positive concept, such as democracy, justice, truth, motherhood, or the American way.

- *Name-calling:* This technique involves an indiscriminate use of labels to encourage the hearer to condemn something or someone without evidence.

- *Plain folks:* A seller may associate his service or product with "most people," or the majority of well-educated, well-informed people. Surveys are often cited in this approach.

- *Testimonial:* A product or concept may be associated with a highly respected (or disliked) personality who advocates the product or concept, in order to encourage its acceptance (or rejection).

When you're in a listening mode, it's important for you to identify whether or not one or more of these approaches is being used in conversation. It's only by looking past others' attempts at persuasion that you can really evaluate the worth of a proposal.

Now let's turn from the qualities of the speaker to the problems that you may be bringing to any verbal exchange.

THE ROADBLOCKS THAT LISTENERS OFTEN ERECT TO SMOOTH COMMUNICATION

It's time for some self-evaluation. Here's a checklist that should help you understand better how you're getting in the way of effective communication by poor listening. These roadblocks you may be erecting to smooth discussion may be divided into three types: stepping out of the listener role; put-downs; and denial of the problem.

The Role Switcher

Do you tend to step out of the listener's role too often? Sometimes you *are* supposed to be the one who's doing the talking, but that's not what we're focusing on here. Our concern is about the time you may be wasting by switching roles with the person you're supposed to be listening to. This problem may emerge in several ways:

- *Ordering, directing, or commanding.* You may tell the other person to do something, or give him an order or command.

- *Advising, giving suggestions, or indicating solutions.* If you tell the other person how to solve the problem you're trying to understand, you're not likely to secure the information you need.

- *Warning, admonishing, or threatening.* This problem may arise if you try to tell the other person what negative consequences will occur if he does or doesn't do something.

- *Moralizing or preaching.* This non-listener tells the other person what he should or ought to do.

- *Persuading, arguing, or lecturing.* The non-listener becomes the seller here, as he tries to influence the other person with facts, counterarguments, piles of information, or a list of opinions.

The Put-Down Artist

This non-listener tends to go on the attack in a number of ways:

- *Judging, criticizing, disagreeing, or blaming.* He makes negative judgments or evaluations of the other person.

- *Inappropriate praise.* This individual offers a positive evaluation or judgment of what the other person has

said *without listening*. Talk about a total waste of
time!

- *Name calling, ridiculing, or shaming.* If you make
the other person feel foolish or uncomfortable, you're
not likely to get any useful information out of him.

The Denier

Those who deny that a problem exists may fail in their
attempts at listening by:

- *Focusing on the person, not the problem.* This poor
listener may try to tell a person what his motives are
or analyze why he is saying what he is. If you give
a person the impression you've "figured him out,"
he'll clam up or become defensive, and certainly
won't dispense freely the information you need.

- *Patronizing or condescending.* This individual tries
to make the other person feel better in a superficial
way, often by denying the strength or validity of the
speaker's concerns.

- *Probing, questioning, interrogating, or placing the
other person on the defensive.* Sometimes, direct,
hard questioning is necessary to get to the heart of a
matter. But if you become too combative when you're
trying to get information, your source will shut down.

HOW TO RECOGNIZE WHERE
COMMUNICATION IS LIKELY
TO BREAK DOWN

The best listeners are especially adept at identifying those
points in a conversation where their ability to listen effectively is most vulnerable. By noting these danger zones
and taking steps to pass safely through them, you'll find
you can strengthen relationships as well as save yourself

a great deal of time. All communications breakdowns occur in one of these six major areas:

AREA #1: PREPARING. Abraham Lincoln said, "I spend one third of my preparation in preparing for what I am going to say, and two thirds of my preparation in anticipating what the other person will say to me." An unprepared listener may be too tired or too distracted to pay attention.

AREA #2: SENSING. You miss the actual words that the speaker used. So if he says a meeting is at 3:30, but you hear 2:30, your entire schedule is going to be thrown for a loop. You may also miss the fleeting facial expressions, gestures, and tone of voice so that if he says 3:30 sarcastically, you may take him seriously. Over 90 percent of the meaning of a spoken message is conveyed non-verbally.

AREA #3: SYNCHRONIZING. You may be "out of sync" with the mood of the speaker. You may have a mismatch in communication style which has resulted in a so-called "personality conflict." Time and emotional energy are expended trying to repair damage that could have been avoided by getting in sync with the speaker.

AREA #4: INTERPRETING. You may hear the actual words of the speaker, but you don't understand them. Four hundred basic words used in eighty percent of our speaking have over sixteen hundred different meanings. If there seems to be any ambiguity in the words, this roadblock may get in the way of effective listening.

AREA #5: EVALUATING. Here the listener must determine what to do with the information given to her. But she may assign the wrong weight to the directions and give too much or too little importance to the task. For example, a manager may be told to finish up an accounting procedure report. But because she is tired and struggling with a problem employee, she gives the order a lower priority—and is chewed out by her boss.

AREA #6: RESPONDING. The listener fails to make an appropriate response to what she's heard. The reasons may include forgetting to do the task, not having enough information, not having enough time, or an inability or lack of skill in executing the work. Effective listeners respond responsibly and raise the self-esteem of the speaker.

To prevent breakdowns of listening and communication in these six areas, one or both of these solutions may work:

• Restate what the speaker wants you to do. You can use the speaker's words, or even better, you can say it in your words, just to be sure you understand.

• Ask *who*, *what*, *when*, *where*, and perhaps *why* or *how*.

In other words, you want to know who should do the task; what exactly has to be done; when the job has to be completed; and where it should be done (unless the answer to this query is obvious). If possible, you should try to find out *why* the task needs to be done and *how* your supervisor or speaker feels it might best be accomplished. These last two bits of information can provide you with a rationale for the work and also make it unnecessary for you to spend time finding out the best procedures for doing the work. Remember, your ultimate objective in going through this effective listening exercise is to save yourself time and to edge closer and closer to the four-hour day. (For those who seek more help on doubling their listening efficiency, we recommend *Listen for Success: A Guide to Effective Listening*, by Arthur Robertson.)

Now you have all the tools you need to achieve the four-hour workday. You've learned how to break through the major time barriers in your life, and you've also explored ways to speed up the important processes of reading, writing, and oral communication. But suppose your boss flatly refuses to honor your quest for the four-hour day? What if the nature of your job, including the demands of clients or colleagues, seems to militate against scaling back so radically on your work time? In short, what good does it do to achieve the four-hour day in theory but not to be able to enjoy it in practice?

We'll confront these and related questions directly in the next chapter.

Chapter Thirteen

The Final Four-Hour Day Frontier: Fighting for Control Over Your Own Time

Suppose you walk into your office tomorrow and announce, "From now on I'm going to work a four-hour day instead of an eight-hour day." How would that go over? The response will depend on what your position is in the organization. Clearly, implementing the four-hour day won't be equally easy for everyone. In fact, no matter who you are, putting these concepts into practice will take some adjustment and considerable rethinking of your schedule and your approach to work. But some variation on the four-hour day is possible in virtually *every* type of work—*if* you're willing to fight for control of your time.

REMEMBER THE PRIME DIRECTIVE

Before we explore the practicalities of putting the four-hour day into effect, keep this principle—what we call the Prime Directive of the Four-Hour Day—in mind: *the four-hour day should be implemented only with tactics that are completely aboveboard and honest.*

It would be easy to use some of the techniques we've been discussing to get all of your work done in four hours and then clandestinely do personal business on company time. That approach, as tantalizing as it may seem at first, will always backfire. If you pursue personal projects during work hours, you should do so only with the knowledge and approval of your supervisor, or in a way that is consistent with company policy. Many companies and professional firms encourage *pro bono publico* work, for instance. This volunteered, unpaid work "for the public good," which promotes worthwhile causes or helps those in need, will often fit nicely into furthering an individual's non-work life priorities.

Now, to understand how the theory of the four-hour day can be put into practice in different work settings, let's turn to a more detailed consideration of the six broad categories of jobs: (1) the small entrepreneur or independent operator; (2) the senior professional; (3) the CEO who, despite his powerful position, must be sensitive to reactions from others in the organization; (4) the manager with some limited control over his time; (5) the heavy-duty junior professional worker; and (6) the nine-to-five type.

The Small Entrepreneur or Independent Operator

Workers in this entrepreneurial category include freelance operatives, independent contractors such as plumbers or handymen, and those who run small businesses such as typing services, small consulting firms, or individual computer services. These people, who have almost total control over their work time, are in an ideal position to implement the four-hour day.

One word of caution: it may be best not to make a public announcement of what you're doing, because a move to cut far down on your work hours can easily be misunderstood. Clients, for instance, may see such a cutback as laziness, a signal of ill health, or a failure to take them and their business seriously.

To reduce the chances of a negative reaction, just play your cards close to the vest. Confide only in those whom you know you can trust, and proceed with your business as usual—with the private understanding that you'll only be working half as many hours each day. If anyone wonders where you are when you're not in the office, a standard, honest response from your secretary or answering service would be that you're "unavailable."

The Senior Professional

The next best situation for having the freedom to implement the four-hour day is probably that of the senior professional, such as a top-level partner in an accounting, law, or consulting firm. If you're in this role, you'll be likely to have the power to set your schedule (and that of those under you) and come and go as you wish. But still, there are often some constraints that may limit your ability to have total control over your schedule:

- The needs and demands of important clients will always carry weight. If a client who regularly pays you high fees tells you there is a pressing issue or emergency to which you must respond by a certain time, then you'll have to respond—or lose the account.

- As the senior person in the organization, you set the tone as a role model. If you seem to be lazy or inattentive to the work, others are likely to follow your example.

- Other senior colleagues may become resentful if they feel you're not pulling your weight. Even if you're a founding partner in the firm, you could be subjecting yourself to considerable criticism.

- If your firm bills by the hour, you could find yourself in a quandary: you're doing more work than you were before, but in less time. How do you justify maintaining your high level of compensation, even though your billable hours are lower than before?

These and related concerns pose some serious questions about the practicalities of putting your four-hour day into effect. Here are some guidelines which may point the way to resolving these problems for the senior professional:

1. START YOUR FOUR-HOUR DAY EARLY. If you encourage or require that other workers be in the office by a certain time, you should be there *before* that time.

2. PICK THE TIMES WHEN YOU CAN WORK MOST EFFICIENTLY AND BE IN THE OFFICE DURING THOSE PERIODS. For example, you may know that you're most productive for the first two hours in the morning and for two hours in the middle of the afternoon. If so, plan to make those your firm, in-the-office work periods.

3. IF YOU CAN PURSUE NON-WORK PROJECTS EFFECTIVELY IN YOUR OFFICE, BY ALL MEANS DO SO. As long as you're at your desk, no one will question the propriety of what you're doing. After all, you're the top boss (or one of the top bosses), and it's your prerogative to pursue those activities that you deem to be important for the future health of the firm. In fact, your involvement in outside projects will probably enhance your value to the organization. It's common for top executives to become leaders in community or volunteer activities because these roles project a positive, altruistic image for the firm.

4. AVOID MAKING CLIENTS NERVOUS. It would be unwise to announce to your clients or customers, "I'm now working four hours a day instead of ten." The first thing that will enter their minds is, "These people are losing their edge. They've lost their drive and commitment to excellence." Instead, just continue to respond to their needs and, if possible, increase the quality of service

you're providing. If you succeed, the question of how much time you're working every day will never arise.

5. IF YOU BILL BY THE HOUR, REVISE THAT PRACTICE AND BILL BY THE JOB OR PROJECT. We realize that this suggestion can be easier said than done, depending on the way your firm calculates its fees. If everyone bills by the hour and you don't, that could throw your accounting department into a quandary. So what should you do?

One possibility is to increase your hourly rates. If you're producing at least the same amount of work, and you're not charging the clients any more, there should be no rational basis for any objections.

A better, though more revolutionary, solution might be to change the billing policy of the entire firm so that you all bill by the job or project, rather than by the hour. Billing by the hour is a destructive practice that over the years has put both the client and the servicing firm at a disadvantage. The clients lose out because many servicing firms tend to pad their hours and as a result may overcharge. The firm loses because its work product may deteriorate as the focus is placed more on time spent than on efficiency and quality of service. With firms that charge by the hour, there will always be a temptation to put in as many hours as possible. The senior partners will work longer because their rates are the highest in the firm; and the associates will compete with one another to see who can bring in the most money on their level. The result will be long hours for everyone, and probably no better result for the client.

So why not just figure out what you need to make as a fee and bill the client for that amount, even if you can do the job by working four-hour days? Some objections to this approach, which will be raised by those experienced in professional work and hourly billings, are: "What happens if I fail to estimate how much a job is really worth?'' Or, ''I can't possibly anticipate what some work is going to cost because my relationship with the client is ongoing. I may be working on a particular case for months or years.''

One possible solution to this dilemma is to estimate by *segments* of a job, billing the client when each segment is completed. Another possibility is to resort to a simple technique mentioned above: just raise your hourly rates. (Of course, if you cut your work time in half, that will mean you'll double your hourly rates— a daunting prospect if you reveal to your client the rate at which you're billing him. In general, it's best not to tell your client what you're charging by the hour and to bill by the job or job segment.)

6. CONSIDER WAYS TO HELP OTHERS IN THE FIRM IMPLEMENT THE FOUR-HOUR-DAY CONCEPT. Remember, you've learned how to be as efficient in half a day as you previously were in an entire day. So why not pass on these insights to others in your firm? Keeping up an acceptable volume of work should be the major objective, not just putting in a certain number of hours. If you can teach them how to do more in less time, you'll have a happier work force and will almost certainly increase your overall productivity.

The Chief Executive Officer

The situation confronting the CEO who desires the four-hour day is usually similar to that of the senior professional—with a few qualifications.

First of all, the senior professional typically owns a substantial interest in his firm, while the CEO, especially one with a publicly held company, is often just an employee. If you own a large stake in your operation, you automatically have more power and authority to do as you please. The CEO, by contrast, may be at the top of the company's hierarchy, but still, he answers to the board. If there is a perception that he isn't pulling his weight, he may be replaced.

Second, even though the CEO possesses tremendous power in decision-making, the corporate culture in large companies is usually determined by some sort of consensus. The CEO may have the most influence of any single individual over the corporate culture; but to operate effectively, he must have the support of others in the organization, especially those who are at the highest executive levels. If he suddenly begins working a different set of hours from everyone else in the company, he'll quickly lose his moral authority and leadership strength.

But even with these limitations, the CEO is in perhaps the strongest position of any of the six types of workers we're discussing to influence large numbers of people to incorporate some version of the four-hour day. If he gradually shapes his schedule to increase his work intensity so that his productivity also increases, he may be able to get other top executives to do the same. If this approach is successful at the highest levels of the company, the executives may be able to design a four-hour-day variation for the organization as a whole. Here are some possibilities:

- Managers and workers at all levels of the organization might focus more on completing projects and assignments in shorter time periods. Emphasizing time-management concepts—such as devising time budgets, breaking through time barriers, and developing work speed skills—would be a major feature of this approach. Finally, working a set number of hours should be *de*emphasized.

- Opportunities should be provided for doing *pro bono* work or certain personal tasks on company time—so long as work assignments are finished first.

- Other incentives might be offered for a high level of efficiency, such as bonuses or time off.

It may be best to implement this kind of program in steps. For example, a company policy might first be established to promote a six-hour workday. Then, if that works, the number of hours could be scaled down again. The workers who succeed in streamlining their work habits and do their assigned jobs in six hours would be given the remaining work time to pursue non-work interests.

The Middle-Level Manager

Unlike the CEO, or even another very senior-level executive, the middle manager has some degree of flexibility and control over his time, *but* he is still very much under the supervision of a boss. Also, like the CEO, he has to be concerned about the kind of role model he is for his subordinates. How can this type of worker enjoy the benefits of the four-hour day? Certainly, he faces a tough challenge. His promotions—indeed, his very job—depend on how his work is evaluated by his supervisors. Appearing to be working less than other people in the office won't go over well. But there are still some possibilities for this type of worker to consider, beginning with an evaluation of current company time-use policies.

You'll have to psyche out your office policy. Before you try to formulate a proposal that could open the door to the four-hour day, you should evaluate how company policy is interpreted and applied in your particular department. If your boss is mainly concerned about whether work is finished on time, and doesn't worry if you have a certain amount of flexibility in your hours, then there may be no problem. On the other hand, your boss may be a stickler for getting into the office at 9:00 A.M., and leaving nothing short of eight or nine hours later. In such a case, you'll have to be more creative in implementing the four-hour day. Here are several ways a manager might be able to achieve this shorter regular workday.

1. RESHAPE YOUR CURRENT JOB. One creative solution would be to negotiate agreements and concessions from

your boss, which, taken together, would produce more productivity.

First, you might point out that you're taking a number of steps, including the development of special time-management strategies, to increase your productivity significantly, and that you'd like some leeway in implementing this personal program. Keep your introduction to your time-management proposal short and general. You'll have plenty of opportunities to get specific later. Until they see the results, many bosses who hear such a proposal will initially be skeptical. In the long run, most will welcome any employee's attempts to become more efficient. Your objective in presenting your case to your employer is to make the most persuasive argument possible.

Second, explain that the primary emphasis of your plan is job or project completion. Give him some specific examples of projects you're now working on or expect to be working on, and estimate the savings in time that you think you can achieve with your new approach. Also, stress the additional things you can accomplish for the company if your personal program works. Tell the boss that you plan to keep him informed in writing about your work goals and that you'll seek feedback from him regularly on your progress.

Third, see if your supervisor is open to the idea of your adopting a more flexible work schedule. You might suggest that you'd like to spend more time out of the office than you have in the past to pursue other client contacts, do independent research, or just stimulate your creative juices. The more specific and well-reasoned you can make your proposal, the more likely it will be that your boss will accept it. Obviously, the more free, unmonitored time you can negotiate, the stronger position you'll be in to achieve a four-hour day.

Fourth, characterize your proposal as a trial, which

can always be dropped if it doesn't work. To this end, set a time limit on your initial efforts, and promise to report your progress back to your boss at the end of the trial period.

Caution: Your proposal cannot be merely a thinly veiled justification for going on a series of boondoggles during work hours. Your program must include sincere attempts to improve your personal creativity and energy and enhance your work productivity. Any suggestions that are little more than an excuse to go to the movies in the middle of the day will be immediately apparent to your boss. The key test will likely be that your suggested out-of-office activity have some clear, identifiable link to your in-office work, or to the company's *pro bono* policy.

At this point, it may be helpful to refer back to the basic life priorities you listed while reading Chapter Three. Anything you can do during your free hours that will support or strengthen those priorities will probably also help refresh your mind and give you new perspectives on problems and situations at work.

2. PROPOSE A NEW JOB. If it doesn't seem possible to reshape your existing job, you may be able to switch jobs within your organization to get responsibilities that fit in better with the four-hour-day concept.

Karen, who was in charge of a large department in a retail chain, decided she wanted to spend more time at home with her young child. She knew that she could do much of her office work more efficiently by applying some of the time-management techniques we've described. At the same time, however, she realized that she had to be on site during office hours to respond to the questions and needs of her staff. Clearly, it wouldn't be workable for her to try to set up a four-hour day while on her present work assignment.

So Karen did some research into other types of jobs that were available in her company, and before long she found two or three that could easily be done at home. These included one that involved the use of computers and telephone communications—skills in which she had expertise. Karen proposed a switch to this more independent work and asked that she be allowed to pursue much of it from her home, through computer and communications hookups. Because she had done such a good job in her management role, her boss recommended her for the position, and soon, she was happily working a four-hour day. She spent most of her time at home, but did come into the office several hours a week to touch base with her new supervisor and other colleagues.

There is a continuing movement to allow this kind of flexible job assignment in various companies, especially for workers who have already proven their reliability in more traditional work settings. You have nothing to lose by exploring such a job change within your organization. With a persuasive written proposal and some appropriate assertiveness with your boss, you may well succeed in finding a position like Karen's.

Of course, none of these approaches may work. If they don't, you'll have one of two other choices:

First, you might rely on four-hour-day principles for *more* than four hours a day. In this way, you will increase your efficiency and productivity to the point that you'll be in a strong position for a promotion—and perhaps a higher-level role that will subsequently enable you to implement some version of the four-hour day.

Second, you may just decide that the inflexibility of your company's policy or supervisors is just too oppressive and that it's time to look for another job. Remember, there are plenty of organizations that are sensitive to the peculiar needs of highly productive workers. If your company isn't in this category, feel free to look elsewhere.

These last two options become especially pertinent as we consider the final two types of workers: the heavy-duty junior professional, and the nine-to-five type.

The Heavy-Duty Junior Professional

The kinds of workers in this category include junior partners and associates in law firms; most physicians and certainly all medical residents; and middle- and even senior-level editorial workers in publishing houses and on periodicals. The *heavy-duty* label applies to anyone with a high level of professional training who has an assigned load of work he must do, even though he seems to have too little time to do it.

The heavy-duty junior professional often finds himself in a bind. On the one hand, he is committed to his work on a long-term career basis, and the traditional way to move up is to work longer and harder than the next guy. On the other hand, he may not want to work those long hours; he may want to work a four-hour day. The catch is that if he decides he's going to leave hours before everyone else, he's not going to be made a partner, or given a promotion, or otherwise be accorded the recognition and high pay that he desires.

1. CHOOSING TO GO OUT, NOT UP. Donald, an extremely bright associate in a big-city law firm, had achieved very high marks and an editorship of the law review in one of the nation's most prestigious law schools. He was one of the first new attorneys hired by his law firm, and great things were expected of him. But there was a problem in this rosy scenario. To begin with, Donald was committed to spending plenty of time with his family. He decided in the first few weeks with the

law firm that he simply couldn't honor his personal values if he worked late into the night and got home after his children were already in bed.

The issue became murkier, however, because it became evident that despite the high quality of legal talent that had been hired by the firm, Donald was the most efficient in doing his work. He could do more than was expected of him in only about five hours a day. The other associates on his level typically put in eleven and twelve hours a day and still accomplished less.

Donald reasoned that if the partner supervising him could look at the situation logically—that is, if the emphasis were on work produced rather than hours spent—he would conclude that it made sense that Donald should be able to leave the office early. Unfortunately, the partner didn't respond logically. "If you don't put in the hours, you won't make partner," he said flatly. So Donald was presented with a choice: either give in to the demands of the firm and reduce the time he spent with his family, or leave the firm. His decision was to leave, and he quickly found a more flexible position in the legal department of a corporation. He also began to prepare to set up a private practice, in which he would be the senior partner who could establish the firm's work style.

2. CHOOSING TO GO UP, NOT OUT. Other heavy-duty junior professionals may take a different path from that selected by Donald. They may decide to stay with their firms and to apply the four-hour-day time-management concepts to increase their productivity to very high levels during a longer workday. In effect, they work one high-intensity four-hour day, and then they immediately embark on *another* four-hour day!

There are some dangers that may accompany this doubling-up of four-hour days: one of the most obvious is that those who work this hard may feel they are right back where they started, or even in a worse position. And usually, they still won't be able to spend extra time with their families, on volunteer tasks, or in other activities that further their basic life priorities. Also, working at a higher level of intensity will be more likely to produce fatigue and exhaustion. If you put in the same number of hours but work harder, you may be so wiped out by the time you return home that you'll find yourself devoting even less time to outside interests.

Yet there are, certainly, some potential advantages to this approach: first of all, some people find that their endurance increases as they work more intensely over an extended period of time. In some ways, the experience is similar to distance running: the more you train, the longer and faster you can go. Also, in many cases working at this high level of intensity does have an end point, or finish line. When many heavy-duty junior professionals secure a promotion, they find they have more control over their time and can ease up or rearrange their work schedules. Of course, if you've spent several years working long hours at a very high intensity, the habit may be so ingrained that it's hard to shift gears and scale back on your work. A kind of addiction to work may result. Also, marriages disintegrate and family relationships deteriorate when heavy-duty professionals begin to emphasize their work over their personal lives.

What approach should you take? It's hard to generalize. Some people do move successfully through a doubling-up phase on their four-hour days and manage to maintain a meaningful life outside of their work. But too often, personal values and relationships suffer. Our advice to the heavy-duty junior professional would be: *always* keep your life priorities at the forefront of your mind every day you go to work. If you find your job getting out of control, or if you begin to see danger signals in your personal life, it's always better to switch jobs than lose a basic value or relationship.

The Nine-to-Five Type

If you're in some other white-collar or blue-collar job that requires you to be in the office without exception on a nine-to-five basis, your options may seem limited. But don't give up on the four-hour day too quickly. There are several ways that you can achieve this working goal if you put your mind to it.

In the first place, you might consider some of the possibilities that have already been described. You could double up on your time by working two consecutive, intense four-hour days every day. This approach would put you in a strong position for promotion to a position that might offer more flexibility.

Another option is to negotiate with your boss for more flexible time, such as work time at home or off the normal job site. These days, there tends to be an increasing emphasis in many businesses on team organization, where a small group of employees band together to do a designated task in the most efficient way they can devise. The emphasis is task-oriented, not hour-oriented. There is a minimum of interference or supervision from the higher-ups, and that leaves plenty of flexibility to work intensely and to free extra time for personal use.

If neither of these routes seems feasible—or palatable— you still have one other way to proceed. You can put in your time on your regular job but in your spare time, prepare to set up your own business. *Many* energetic, efficient, creative nine-to-fivers have established successful enterprises that give them complete control and flexibility over their workdays. We know numerous people who have gone from clerical or other closely supervised positions to such independent ventures as:

- Typing and word-processing services
- Computer repair and consulting services

- House painting
- Construction and restoration work
- Independent sales positions, such as representatives for telephone services, office equipment, and delivery systems
- Agents and brokers for insurance, mutual funds, or investment vehicles

The list could go on and on, but the main message is just to be aware of the wide variety of opportunities that become available to you when you streamline your use of time after work.

In a nutshell, here's a game plan you might follow if you decide you'd like to go off on your own and achieve the freedom to institute a four-hour day:

1. Do some research on possible entrepreneurial ventures that might work for you.
2. Choose one, and set aside forty-five minutes every evening to work on it. The chances are, when you really get rolling, you'll spend more than forty-five minutes, but three quarters of an hour is a good initial goal.
3. Establish a time limit to complete your planning and actually get started on your venture.
4. When you begin to pursue your independent work, do it part-time at first. Continue to work at your old job. This approach will provide you with a kind of insurance policy, or a fallback position, just in case your entrepreneurial goals don't work out the way you've planned.
5. When you've built up your outside business so that it provides at least a steady 60 to 75 percent of the personal income you need, consider quitting your regular job and devoting yourself full-time to your new venture.

As you can see, there are many potential uses for the four-hour-day concept. You will most likely have to fight—and fight hard—to put it into effect in your daily life. No radical change comes without some significant adjustment in your outlook, schedule, and relationships. But when you achieve the goal, there will be no doubt in your mind that the personal revolution you've experienced has been worth it.

Chapter Fourteen

Why This Is Not a Time-Management Book

The four-hour day involves more than just learning and implementing a number of time-saving techniques. That's why we have emphasized several times that this book is not primarily concerned with time management. Rather, we're urging you to bring about a true *revolution* in the way you live each day.

Before you ever begin to work toward a four-hour day, it's essential to decide *why* you want it. Otherwise, it's likely that your enthusiasm and resolve to see your objectives through to a successful conclusion will fade. Without a clear understanding of your goals, you are likely to find your commitment overwhelmed by challenges such as these:

- The dislocations that always accompany radical changes in your daily schedule.

- The high level of creativity required for an evaluation and reordering of your life.

- Inevitable opposition from peers, supervisors, and clients as you try to put the four-hour day into practice.

What we've been talking about in these pages is not just a means of getting more time, but rather a way to achieve your dearest values and goals. The four-hour day is a system that can finally put you on the track to finding true meaning in life—while giving your work and leisure greater significance. There's no point to continuing in a rut that leads you toward goals that mean little or nothing to you. You've reevaluated your life priorities; you're clear about what your fundamental values are; and you know several ways to achieve them. The time has arrived to act on this knowledge. There's no point in being unhappy, stressed out, and unfulfilled. Life is too short.

Granted, there are risks involved in embarking on a program that will culminate in a four-hour workday. But if you think about it, the risks are even greater if you fail to take this path. Unless you reorganize your schedule so that much of your time is devoted to achieving your major life priorities, you'll find, years hence, that you've been moving far afield from your goal. In fact, you may find that the time is so late and you're so removed from your original aspirations, it seems impossible to get back on the track. You may worry that now there's no chance to make your life count for something.

But we're optimists. We believe it's *never* too late to embark on a path to the four-hour day—and in the process, to transform your very existence. It's just a matter of getting started by taking those first few steps that we outlined at the beginning of this book. Once you know what your fundamental priorities are (or should be) and make a firm commitment to fulfilling them, you will have turned a corner. You'll be well on your way to changing forever your understanding not only of time, but of life itself.

Achieving the four-hour day will certainly take more thought and effort for some people than for others, primarily because jobs, values, and relationships vary widely. But ultimately, the goal of making work hours shorter *and* higher in quality is attainable for anyone. The secret to ongoing success is to continue to approach time not as a rigid, fixed series of minutes and hours, but rather, as a dynamic dimension of reality that exists not to control you but to serve your best interests.

BUILD YOUR OWN BUSINESS LIBRARY

with the

21ST CENTURY ENTREPRENEUR SERIES!

HOW TO OPEN A FRANCHISE BUSINESS
Mike Powers   77912-9/$12.50 US/$16.00 Can

HOW TO OPEN YOUR OWN STORE
Michael Antoniak   77076-8/$12.50 US/$15.00 Can

HOW TO START A HOME BUSINESS
Michael Antoniak   77911-0/$12.50 US/$16.00 Can

HOW TO START A SERVICE BUSINESS
Ben Chant and Melissa Morgan
                                77077-6/$12.50 US/$15.00 Can